Prais

Domestic abuse impacts one in four women in America, and families in the faith community are no exception. Everyone has a role to play in creating peaceful families, especially people of faith. High-profile domestic violence cases in the media raise public awareness, yet domestic abuse is more often characterized by the largely overlooked and unreported low-profile cases going on every day.

Rose Saad adds her thoughtful voice to the timely discussion of domestic abuse. Her book is interspersed with meaningful first-hand accounts and extremely practical advice, both for the abused person and her faith community. She has made a valuable contribution to an important cultural conversation.

Rev. Zeke Wharton
Pastor, Inspiration Community Church
Past President, Interfaith Community Against Domestic Violence

Rose Saad has written a courageous book, as one who has been through one of life's toughest storms. Domestic violence, and its carnage, is misunderstood—especially in the church. It's time for the church to wade into these deep waters and offer abuse victims the protection they deserve. God has always been concerned about the oppressed. "God is close to the broken hearted" (Psalm 34:18 NIV).

Steven D. Brand, MSW/MPH, LCSW, ACSW

A PATH TO HOPE

RESTORING
THE SPIRIT OF
THE ABUSED
CHRISTIAN
WOMAN

ROSE SAAD

A Path to Hope

Copyright© 2016 by Rose Saad

All rights reserved. No part of this book may be reproduced in any form without permission in writing from the publisher, except in the case of brief quotations embodied in critical articles or reviews.

Published by
Deep River Books
Sisters, Oregon
www.deepriverbooks.com

Scripture quotations marked with NLT are taken from *The Holy Bible*, New Living Translation, copyright 1996, 2004, 2007. Used by permission of Tyndale House Publishers, Inc., Carol Stream, Illinois 60188. All rights reserved.

Scripture quotations marked with NIV are taken from *The HOLY BIBLE*, NEW INTERNATIONAL VERSION. Copyright 1973, 1979, 1984 by International Bible Society. Used by permission of Zondervan. All rights reserved.

Scripture quotations marked *The Message* are taken from THE MESSAGE. Copyright 1993, 1994, 1995, 1996, 2000, 2001, 2002. Used by permission of NavPress Publishing Group.

Scripture quotation marked ESV is from the ESV® Bible (The Holy Bible, English Standard Version®), copyright © 2001 by Crossway, a publishing ministry of Good News Publishers. Used by permission. All rights reserved.

Scripture quotation marked GNT is from the Good News Translation® (Today's English Version, Second Edition) Copyright © 1992 American Bible Society. All rights reserved.

ISBN: 9781940269818
Library of Congress: 2016935473

Cover design by Robin Black, Inspirio Design

Published in the USA

CONTENTS

Acknowledgments..9
Introduction..11

PART ONE: The Abused Woman................................21
1. *A Christian Woman's Journey Through Domestic Violence*..........23
   The Beginning / The Marriage / The Church
2. *The Dynamics of Domestic Violence* 41
   Tactics the Abuser Uses to Maintain and Achieve Control / Power and Control Wheel / "The Cycle of Violence" (as developed by Lenore Walker) / Impact of the Abuse on the Woman / Denial: The Glue That Binds / Reasons Why She Stays

PART TWO: Digging Into the Scriptures 57
3. *Spiritual Dilemmas*..59
   Abandonment by God / The Nature of Suffering / The Value of Obedience / Biblical Justification for Separation and Divorce
4. *What Does the Scripture Say?* 77
   Domestic Violence as Sin / So Who Is Responsible? / Examining the Scriptures about Relationships

PART THREE: Lessons for Healing 95
5. *Choosing to Heal and Hope Again*..........................97
   Self-Evaluation / The Power Is in the Choice (Healing Is a Choice)/ Hopeless Versus Hope in God
6. *Is This Love?* 113
   What Is Love and What Love Is Not / God is Love / Embracing God's Love

7. *Doing the Work: Anger, Forgiveness, and Grieving*..............139
   Dealing with Anger / Forgiveness Is a Process / Grieving: The Act of Letting Go

PART FOUR: The Community 173
8. *How Can The Community Help the Abused Christian Woman?* 175
   Myths about Domestic Violence / How to Help / How the Church Can Help
9. *Sexual Violence Against Women in the Bible and How the Community Responded*..193
   Dinah / Tamar / The Levite and His Concubine / Some Facts about Sexual Assault within Marriage

Afterword 211
Notes 215
Resources..221
Connect with the Author 222

This book is dedicated to the Christian woman who is trying to make sense of her abusive relationship. May God bless you with his wisdom and knowledge as you seek clarity and healing from the bondage of domestic violence. May he fill you with joy and peace as you trust in him so that you may overflow with hope by the power of the Holy Spirit (Romans 15:13, NIV).

ACKNOWLEDGMENTS

I extend my deepest gratitude to Kathy Brown-Huamani, who spent countless hours not only editing and guiding how I organized my ideas, but also encouraging me along the way to complete the project.

I also wish to thank Shawna Rodenberg for going above and beyond the call of duty in helping me to restructure the book.

Thanks also to Barbara Manuputy for her encouragement and careful review of the book.

Special thanks to Cora Spaulding, my friend and encourager, for her continued love and support over the years.

To all my sisters in Christ, who believe in me and who played some role in the preparation and completion of the book. I will forever be thankful.

Above all, I want to thank the women who survived domestic violence and were willing to share their stories. I am honored to know them.

And I am filled with gratitude for our Lord and Savior, my Counselor, powerful God, Everlasting Father, and Prince of Peace.

INTRODUCTION

Even among trained professionals, a woman who experiences domestic violence is frequently misunderstood. I observed this problem working as an emergency room nurse for more than twenty years. On many occasions I have seen police officers react cynically and in a condescending manner toward a brutally beaten woman brought to the hospital for emergency care. This was especially true when the woman refused to press charges. Healthcare professionals and even the woman's own family members and friends would refer to her as "mentally unstable," "co-dependent," or "dumb."

When I began to recognize that I, too, was a victim of domestic abuse, which occurred in the latter part of my relationship, I developed a greater compassion for and understanding of the domestic violence victims I saw in the ER. I began to recognize that, although the behaviors of these women appeared irrational, the reality was that they were trying to make sense of what was happening.

As I reflect on my relationship, most of my ten years of marriage was spent trying to make sense of what was happening at home. My husband's behaviors were confusing. Many hours of my day were spent pounding my thoughts to make sense of his abusive behaviors toward me and to find ways to minimize them. After outbursts of verbal abuse and at times physical abuse, I longed for a clear explanation for his abusive actions. Often I left our communications feeling guilty and I assumed the responsibility for his behaviors, subsequently evaluating my own actions. Did I use the right tone of voice? Did I disregard his request? Or was I disrespectful during the communication process that led to the angry outburst? I wanted reasons to justify his abusive behaviors. The more I wanted to make sense of what was happening, the more I felt controlled by his behaviors.

Not only were his actions confusing, they were also unpredictable. For instance, he would exhibit loving and kind behavior during a normal interaction, but without any warning signs, a few minutes later, he would become irritable and hostile. This unpredictability affected my behavior. I withdrew from my friends and family to discourage them from coming to visit. I couldn't predict if he would be hospitable or avoid interacting with them. His mood and disposition created an elephant in the room. I found myself filled with anxiety, fully expecting an explosion at any moment.

His unpredictability also affected my physical state. For example, I remember coming home each day from work, and as I approached my driveway, my body automatically would switch into a fright mode. Palpitations, a queasy sensation in my stomach, and tension in my muscles were some of the symptoms I experienced because I wasn't sure what to expect when I opened the door. All these behaviors contributed to an overwhelming sense of anxiety, fear, and helplessness that affected my self-esteem. I did not like who I was becoming, and that played a role in influencing my decision to seek change.

My desire for answers to make sense of the abuse was also evident in my relationship with God. I often prayed, "Is my abuse my cross to bear?" "Are my sins stopping my husband from changing?" I went to the church wanting answers from the scriptures. The scriptures used to help me often created more confusion than clarity. Scriptures like "love covers the multitude of sins" (1 Peter 4:8), created more confusion than clarity. Is accepting abuse a demonstration of love? I needed answers to my questions.

I was fortunate to have brothers and sisters in Christ who did not have all the answers but who, nevertheless, offered emotional and physical support. They were willing to listen to my story even though at times, my thoughts were fragmented and didn't make sense. As I look back, I am thankful for them because they listened to and believed my story. The love and support I received strengthened me to make the right choice and take the necessary steps to break free from the abuse.

Even though I left the abuse, I needed emotional and spiritual healing. I sought support from the secular community because no formal, faith-based support program existed in my area. Although the secular support groups helped me to feel less isolated by introducing me to women who, like me, were seeking to make sense of the violence they had experienced, I quickly realized that I would need to look elsewhere to find spiritual healing.

Alone, I wrestled with God and dug deep into his Word to gain wisdom and to understand my experience with domestic violence. This personal struggle brought me to a deeper understanding of God's character and he became the center of my quest for healing. I went to him for the strength that I needed. I made him my own "Counselor," "Mighty God," and "Prince of Peace." His word served as the catalyst for changing my perception of the situation I found myself in (and my perception of myself). This process ultimately led to a discovery of God's power to free me from the emotional and spiritual effects of my abuse.

My own spiritual healing process inspired in me a deep desire to help other Christian women use the Word of God to understand what had happened to them and to gain freedom from the emotional and spiritual bondage that comes from domestic abuse. I began by planning and organizing a support group within my own faith community and then expanded the group to include Christian women from other faith communities. In the process, I created written material to help guide our discussions as well as to help women navigate the scriptures to find encouragement and clarity. In the process of developing the material for the support group, I realized that women and faith communities in other locations could benefit from this material. So began my idea for writing a book about the Christian woman and domestic violence.

I believe this book can be used as a guide for the abused Christian woman and her faith community as she seeks help and healing from spousal abuse. The goal is to help the woman gain a better understanding of her internal conflicts, clarify the scriptures that often lead to spiritual dilemmas, find peace with the decision she makes to break free from abuse, and achieve healing by studying the scriptures and applying them to her situation.

I also believe that this book can serve as a guide for the faith community. The community will gain new awareness by learning to understand the abused woman's behaviors and why she thinks the way she does. They will come to understand her internal conflicts and spiritual struggles as she seeks freedom from abuse and seeks healing. Understanding the abused woman and the impact of the violence is essential to effectively helping her to seek change. The role of the faith community is to help build the woman's faith, clarify her spiritual conflicts, provide referral to appropriate resources, and to hold their abusive members accountable.

I have divided the book into four Parts. Part One, "The Abused Woman" (Chapters 1–2); Part Two, "Digging Into the Scriptures" (Chapters 3–4); Part Three, "Lessons for Healing" (Chapters, 5–7); and Part Four, "The Community" (Chapters 8–9).

Personal stories from Christian women who survived domestic abuse are used to validate the text. These women were willing to share their pain so that other abused women could gain comfort in knowing that they are not alone. It took courage, strength and vulnerability for these women to expose raw emotions that some may have difficulty comprehending. Nevertheless, it is their truth and it has to be told to set others free. What Paul states in 2 Corinthians 12:10, "For when I am weak I am strong," is evident in the stories of these women. Through their own spiritual journeys they were empowered by the scriptures to change their situation. God used the dark moments of their lives for his glory.

Part One focuses on the abused woman's experience. Chapter 1, "A Christian Woman's Journey through Domestic Violence," is my story, intertwined with the story of abused Christian women that I encountered in the church, secular support groups, and as a facilitator for a faith-based support group. Collectively, I hope our stories will awaken the conscience of the reader to recognize that the Christian abused woman's story is her story, the story of her mother, sister, a member of her congregation, or friend.

On her journey through abuse, the woman reveals her conflicts and confusions about her husband's behaviors and her response to those behaviors. She explains how she sought to understand the reasons for her husband's abusive actions and her attempts to minimize those behaviors. As the relationship deteriorates, transformation occurs. She describes how she recognizes that she is losing her sense of self. She does not like who she has become, but feels powerless to change her situation.

She comes to the church seeking understanding and support. She wants others to validate that her husband's behaviors are destroying the family. She thinks that if her husband seeks help and changes, the marriage will be saved. Instead, the interpretation of the scriptures by those who are trying to help her creates more confusion. Her confusion affects her relationship with God. God and the scriptures become a source of confusion and conflict instead of the source of peace they were intended to be.

Education is the first step to breaking free. Chapter 2, "The Dynamics of Domestic Abuse," describes the types of domestic violence, the cycle of violence, the power and control wheel, and the impact of violence on the woman. The chapter also discusses the role of denial in an abusive relationship and the reasons why the woman might choose to stay in the relationship. The abused woman and those who are willing to help her must educate themselves about domestic violence and be aware of the resources in the community to effectively help her seek change.

Part Two, "Digging Into the Scriptures," focuses on the Christian abused woman's response to the scriptures and the conflicting advice she receives from her community, as well as, how the scriptures view violence. The woman discloses her sense of confusion that complicates her journey and creates a spiritual dilemma. These spiritual conflicts or dilemmas stem from a sense of abandonment by God, questions about the reasons for suffering and the value of submission, and possibly the need to justify separation or divorce. She questions her faith in God because her husband does not change his abusive behaviors. In fact she thinks her faith will cause her husband to stop his abusive behaviors. Chapter 3, "Spiritual Dilemmas," discusses scriptures that contribute to her spiritual dilemmas. The purpose of the discussion is to help the abused woman confront misconceptions about the scriptures and to help her gain clarity as she attempts to apply them to her situation. The goal is to help the woman develop her own convictions and to be comfortable with the decision she makes to stay or leave her abusive relationship.

Chapter 3, "What Does the Scripture Say?" focuses on sinful behaviors of the abuser and how God responds to those behaviors. Knowing how God responds to violence will promote comfort and healing rather than guilt for the woman. Included in this chapter are the stories of Abigail and Sarah, women that the abused woman is called to imitate. The purpose of these stories is to help each woman develop her own convictions about these women, and to help her change her perceptions about her relationship and the abuse.

Healing is a choice and it is essential for breaking free from the effects of domestic abuse. Part Three, "Lessons for Healing," includes Chapters 5 through 7. All chapters in Part Three look at scriptures that can heal some of the emotions that have kept the Christian abused women—even those who have left their relationships—in the bondage of abuse. Each lesson includes a section titled "Self-Reflection," with questions to help the woman discover how the scriptures can be applied to her situation. At the end of each lesson are additional scriptures to encourage the woman to immerse herself in the Word of God.

The studies in Part Two in no way substitute for individual therapy or support groups conducted by a licensed professional. The woman who is recovering from abuse may need professional help from Christian or secular counselors. Peer support groups, either at domestic violence centers or churches, are essential. In these groups, the abused woman will meet other women who have had experiences similar to hers and who can validate those experiences. Validation of her experience is empowering and frees the abused woman from thinking that she is crazy.

Chapter 4, "Choosing to Heal and Hope Again," focuses on making the choice to heal and regain hope in God. The chapter begins with a discussion of self-evaluation. To start the healing process, the woman must consider what initiated and sustained her abusive relationship. As she makes the choice to heal, she must take personal responsibility for changing what she can and letting go of what is not her responsibility. The chapter concludes with a discussion of hope. The abused woman must relearn hope and trust in God's promises as she embarks on her healing process.

Chapters 5, "Is This Love?" attempts to help the woman reconsider her understanding of what love is. The abused woman must recognize that her definition of love needs to change because the experience of abuse has altered her view of love. This chapter discusses what love is and what love is not. The woman learns to redefine love by considering how God loves. The chapter concludes with the acceptance of God's love. The abused woman needs to learn to embrace God's love so that she can love him, herself, and others in the way that God desires.

Chapter 6, "Doing the Work: Anger, Forgiveness, and Grieving," focuses on the process of dealing with anger, forgiving, and grieving the experience of abuse. To heal, it is critical that the abused Christian woman gets in touch with her anger and that she finds healthy ways to express and manage it. She must gain a new understanding of forgiveness and use that knowledge to forgive others and herself. The woman also needs to realize that grieving is part of the process of healing from an abusive relationship. Grieving this type of relationship involves much more the grieving of losses associated with separation or divorce.

The Word of God has the power to heal. When healing is done, the woman is no longer an abused woman, but a *conqueror* of domestic abuse. My prayer is that this part of the book will become a stepping-stone for freeing each reader from the effects of her abuse. Again, always keep in mind that change takes time, patience, and hard work.

The last section, Part Four, focuses on the role of the community as the woman seeks assistance and healing. The "community" means those who are willing to help the Christian woman, and includes family, friends, Christian brothers and sisters, hot-line staff, domestic violence centers, and the church (e.g., church leaders, spiritual advisors, mentors, and counselors). Part Four concludes with a call to respond. It is important to note that violence against women is not an accepted behavior by God's people. It violates the woman, the family, and God's laws. Part Four ends with the emphasis, as part of God's people, we have the moral responsibility and are called *to respond* to stop violence against women and hold the perpetrators accountable for their acts of violence.

Those who wish to help the abused woman must evaluate their beliefs or perceptions about domestic violence. Chapter 8 "How Can the Community Help the Abused Christian Woman?" presents the myriad of myths about domestic violence that lead to misconceptions about the abused woman and hinders the community from effectively helping her.

Specific steps to help the abused woman are discussed. Some typical behaviors of the abuser also are discussed. Recognizing typical abusive behaviors and the manipulative tactics used by the abuser is critical to effectively helping families experiencing domestic violence.

The chapter concludes with a discussion of how the church can help. The discussion begins by clarifying the thinking of the abused Christian woman. Those within the church who are willing to help the woman must understand how the abuse has had an effect on her thinking and perception. She comes to the church seeking clarity, validation and physical, psychological, and spiritual support. The church community must recognize and respect the courage required for the abused woman to seek help in the first place. Scriptures and stories from an abused Christian woman are presented to help clarify ways that the church can support the woman and minimize her confusion. There are suggestions from the abused woman and a pastor on how to help.

In Chapter 9, "Sexual Violence against Women in the Bible and How the Community Responded," the stories of Dinah (Genesis 31:1–31), Tamar (2 Samuel 13:1–39), The Levite and his Concubine (Judges 19:1–30 and Judges 20:1–48) are discussed. These stories do not directly relate to marital violence (most deal with sexual assault), but demonstrate the community response to violence against women in the Bible. These stories demonstrate how the families and the community held the perpetrators accountable for their acts of violence against women.

The chapter emphasizes a theme of the whole book, namely that stopping violence against women and holding perpetrators accountable begins within the family and continues within the church community.

Paul states, "All praise to God, the Father of our Lord Jesus Christ. God is our merciful Father and the source of all comfort. He comforts us in all our troubles so that we can comfort others. When they are troubled, we will be able to give them the same comfort God has given us" (2 Corinthians 1:3, NLT). I am compelled by this scripture to share my pain and the comfort I received from God during my healing so that others may receive the same comfort and move forward to break free from the bondage of domestic abuse. I pray that those who read this book will develop a new awareness of how to help the Christian woman as she travels through her journey to overcome abuse.

CHAPTER 1

A CHRISTIAN WOMAN'S JOURNEY THROUGH DOMESTIC VIOLENCE

The woman's story is a combination of stories drawn from women within the church and participants of secular and faith-based support groups. The story illustrates the dynamics of domestic violence and will help the reader to better understand the Christian woman on her journey through domestic violence.

During the early phase of the woman's journey, she is unaware that she is in an abusive relationship and that her husband's abusive behaviors are tactics used to establish control. For example, she may not notice that his insults and name-calling are designed to destroy her self-confidence, or that his attempts to create conflicts with her family, friends, and other sources of support are intended to socially isolate her. By isolating her, he makes her more dependent on him.

The woman's actions and emotions described in the story reveal her response to the abuse. Her feelings and behaviors are typical of women experiencing abuse. When the woman finally comprehends that she is experiencing domestic violence, the impact of the abuse has infected her physical, emotional, and spiritual wellbeing. She is overwhelmed by anxieties and fears, which consume her daily life and affect her ability to think through her options and make decisions to seek change. She also is preoccupied with trying to avoid the abuse, which depletes energy needed for carrying out her normal life functions.

The woman's story continues with her experience in the church as she seeks help. She is exhausted, confused about her husband's abusive behaviors and she desperately needs others' support and guidance. Instead, she is presented with advice and scriptures that create more confusion.

The Beginning

She meets "Mr. Right." He is intelligent, charming, sociable, and an immaculate dresser. During the dating period, he takes her on long walks, holding hands, and calls constantly just to say he is thinking about her. He is affectionate, thoughtful, listens to her stories, and sends her flowers. He appears to have strong morals and values and is a hard worker with a clear plan for the future. Mr. Right tells her his dreams and aspirations. He listens to her dreams and aspirations. During the early stages of the relationship, he brings up the idea of marriage.

According to him, he has been looking for the right woman for a while and she is that woman. The feeling is mutual. She feels that she also has found Mr. Right.

However, she begins to experience some nagging, uncomfortable feelings about his behavior, but she suppresses them. For example, he talks about past sexual relationships in intimate detail and asks her about details of her past sexual relationships. She finds that type of probing uncomfortable. She notices he expresses excessive anger when he talks about certain family members or old girlfriends. He also has no close or meaningful friendships. He does not trust people. He makes comments such as, "You cannot trust anyone but yourself," and "People are out to get you." He calls at odd hours "just to check in" or may just show up at her job or other places unannounced. He justifies his behaviors by saying, "I can't be away from you," or "I had to hear your voice."

She begins to notice his aggressive tendencies. For example, when driving, he uses abusive language in response to minor infractions by other drivers and sometimes threatens them. Most importantly, he seems unable to resolve conflicts. He never states the reasons for his anger or discusses the feelings that might have led him to react with anger in certain situations. He also fails to take responsibility for his own behavior and always seems to blame others for the problems in his life.

NANCY

HE WAS STANDING on a ladder hanging stage lights on the stage and he seemed really nice. I had to walk back and forth on the stage and he was so funny-acting, like I was doing it on purpose just to see if he would notice me. I thought he was good-looking and funny (a real charmer). We were both volunteering at a benefit for Domestic Violence. (I thought this made him safe and a good candidate for me, as I had grown up with domestic violence and had boyfriends that also were violent.) Each night during the shows, I was the one giving him directions. He was over ten years older and seemed very interested in me. I soon accepted his offer for dinner and he convinced me to come to the city where he lived, since we did not have another show for several days. We lived in separate cities and were both very busy, traveling for work. He would often want extra attention on the phone and ask for more and more details of my exact whereabouts. He sometimes just showed up, which I found weird since he lived in another city. He became more possessive of me, wanting me to go everywhere with him, even when it made no sense or upset others. He seemed to just get away with bending rules. I thought at the time that it was a good thing, that he wanted me with him all the time.

The Marriage

Early in the marriage, the woman begins to notice a change in her husband's behavior. He is withdrawn and temperamental at times. He also is emotionally unpredictable. One moment he is happy, the next he is sad or angry (Jekyll and Hyde personality).

He leaves home for hours and is evasive about his whereabouts, but interrogates her when she is out without him. He calls her multiple times during the day to see where she is and what she is doing. He also scrutinizes her telephone calls. He creates conflict with her closest friends by telling her they were "hitting" on him. He accuses her friends of having "loose or perverse morals." He also makes disparaging remarks about her family members. He may be nice to them when they are around; but when they leave, he criticizes them. According to him, she should not trust others, not even her friends and family (by implication, she should trust only him). He does not tell her when her family and friends call and is rude on the phone or hangs up on them. He behaves in ways that make her family and friends uncomfortable so that they reduce calls and visits. For example, he withdraws or barely speaks to family members when they visit. Or he behaves in inappropriate ways around them, such as getting drunk. She makes excuses for his behaviors and finds herself discouraging visits from friends and family to decrease the tension that he creates when they are around. As her friends and family withdraw, she finds herself with minimal support, which leads to physical and emotional isolation.

NANCY

WE GOT MARRIED in an empty church. He did not like most of my friends, so none were invited. He did not have any friends come nor did we ever spend time with his friends. What I thought was a friendship of his was just a business relationship. Our wedding night was the farthest thing from a dream coming true unless a nightmare is included in that. That night altered my mind in such an incredibly powerful way. The next several years offered moments of pure hell as I tried to even out the rollercoaster that was our marriage and have some semblance of normalcy. I would never be "normal" again.

DEBBIE

I REMEMBER COMING BACK from the honeymoon and asking my husband, "Aren't you going to carry me over the threshold?" He looked at me and said, "You better walk over here, girl." He walked into the apartment and closed the door and left me standing outside. I stood there for a minute or two and eventually walked into the house. A little piece of me died at that moment. The next day my girlfriend called and she said, "God is good" and asked, "How was it?" I said, "God is good." I couldn't tell her the truth. I didn't want to share my disappointment with other Christian women because I didn't want to discourage them. Christian women save themselves for the wedding night so it can be great and pure. I felt like sharing my bad experience would cause a single Christian woman who is saving herself for marriage to "slip on a banana peel." I told my girlfriend everything was great and fabulous. I shut down and pretended that everything was OK.

Every time you lie, a little part of you dies. I prided myself in my honesty. I loved having a clear conscience—no secrets. After becoming a Christian, what I had longed for was a peaceful place where there are no secrets and everything is out on the table.

According to Patricia Evans, author of *Verbal Abuse Survivors Speak Out*, in the normal communication process, an individual comes with an end goal in mind. That intent or end goal is clear. The communicator wants the receiver to do something, agree, or disagree with the verbal or non-verbal message. What a person says and does is in harmony with his or her intent or end goals.[1]

The abused Christian woman's husband's communication creates confusion and conflict. His motives are not clear during the communication process. Inconsistency exists between what he says he wants her to do and his response when she does what she believes he wants. For example, he tells her to look pretty for a party and, when she dresses up, he accuses her of trying to pick up another man. Or, during what she thinks are normal conversations; he suddenly finds something she says offensive (e.g., implying that she wants to cheat or that she is belittling him). As a result of his misinterpretation of her words and actions, she questions her own motives and behaviors.

His communication is also contradictory. For example, he says to her, "I love you," then, a few hours later, he verbally abuses her, calling her names. She wonders, "If he says he loves me, why does he treat me in such a manner?"

He often uses normal expressions of love to belittle and demean her. For example, birthdays and specials occasions that are important to her are intentionally forgotten, or presents are given but later taken away or destroyed when he is angry. Or, he refuses to help with childcare or household duties when she is exhausted or ill.

She wants to believe he loves her, even though his behaviors don't reflect loving actions. Over time she compromises her definition of love and accepts his unloving behaviors while holding on to any gesture of intimacy as evidence of his love for her. For example, she associates his desire for sex as proof that he loves her. She thinks, "Since he wants sex, it must mean he still loves me."

He increasingly invalidates and belittles her feelings and opinions. For example, he may say, "You make a big deal out of everything," or "That doesn't make any sense." He gradually withdraws expressions of affection or perverts his acts of affection in ways that embarrass and humiliate her (e.g., he touches her in inappropriate ways when others are around or in public). He demands sex any time he wants regardless of her feelings. He often makes a point of ridiculing her ideas, explaining why her values are wrong or unimportant. He also stops seeking her input and begins making decisions without her consent, such as, buying expensive household items, so that she gradually finds that she has very little input into major family decisions. These actions disrespect her needs and invalidate her feelings, causing her to feel inadequate or unintelligent.

Her husband blames her for problems in the relationship and household. For example, he blames her for their kids' bad behaviors but refuses to accept any responsibility for childcare. Or, he blames her for financial difficulties, although she has little real input into financial decisions. He also makes her feel that she is at fault for every conflict, but is unwilling to accept any resolution she proposes. Even when he has fits of rage and/or verbally or physically abuses her, he will pass the blame to her by making comments like, "If you had not provoked me, I would not have called you those names," or "You talk too much and needed to be taught a lesson."

The constant blame leads to an increasing feeling of guilt and sense of failure and hopelessness while releasing him from any responsibility for his bad behavior.

She wants him to stop his abusive behaviors and thinks that if she performs certain tasks, he will be nice to her or at least performing these tasks will prevent an explosion of temper. She engages in "performance love" because she believes "If I do everything to please him, he will feel loved and then love me." She finds herself constantly performing task after task, even though her husband's behavior toward her doesn't change. For example, he verbally abuses her because the house is not clean enough. So she cleans the house thoroughly and his only response is another complaint like, "You look terrible; why don't you fix yourself up once in a while?" It now seems that she is constantly doing what he wants, but there is no change in his behaviors toward her.

As her self-esteem is destroyed and confusion about her husband's behaviors increases, she questions her own thoughts and behaviors. She cannot understand why her husband makes cruel remarks or physically attacks her; over time, she begins to accept that she must have done something wrong to trigger those behaviors.

As she increasingly feels confusion, guilt, and low self-worth because of her husband's behaviors, she also begins to fear for her physical safety and the safety of her loved ones. He instills fear by threatening or inflicting physical pain or injury, making traumatizing insults or accusations, or actually taking away or withholding something she needs or values greatly, humiliating her before others, or threatening or inflicting suffering on loved ones. She dreads these types of consequences and tries to avoid them, losing her sense of control and thus giving him a tool for controlling her behaviors as well as her emotions.

She fears his anger, and her fear is increased by his unpredictability. She does not know what will set him off. Her fear reaches its highest peak when he becomes critical or withdrawn, temperamental, or cold and distant, causing her to "walk on eggshells." She knows that there is going to be an explosion, but she does not know when. Her body also recognizes an impending threat and incites the "fight or flight" response. This response causes an increase in her heart rate, a queasy sensation in her stomach, headaches, tense muscles, and difficulty sleeping. She feels paralyzed, trapped, and confused about what to do. She also feels exhausted and overwhelmed.

Not knowing when he will release his violent actions causes prolonged physical and emotional stress. At times, it is easier to provoke him to get over with the violence in order to gain some sense of control. Constant exposure to this kind of fear is paralyzing and depletes her ability to manage her life.

NANCY

RIGHT BEFORE I HAD OUR THIRD BABY, he choked me as I sat in a chair. He did this during sex, too, but I was too ashamed to talk about it. I was often confused and learned to wait—maybe he'd be nice again soon. During conversation I would be ignored or treated like I should know better than to ask right now. We moved from state to state so I could never really feel grounded and I was denied my family. And I felt like no one even knew who I was before all the abuse, so they would not know how different I had become. It became almost automatic to ignore a situation. After an abusive incident, the next morning I would wake up and go make the coffee and it would be like nothing ever happened. I would hang pictures over holes on walls and posters over doors. I would sweep up glass and throw away furniture broken by my body. I started to have bouts of out-of-body experiences during the abuse. I would just want to sleep more and more and not move. I would panic before he came home, I couldn't sleep. Sometimes I couldn't eat. I was too afraid to make a choice without him. I would ask him which he wanted, before opening a can of green beans or corn, making myself believe that if I did this then perhaps he would not get mad. My mind was going quickly. I lost a lot of independence as my health became more impaired. I also tried psychiatric medications to help me to "fix" the marriage. And lost more of who I was.

DEBBIE

NOT TOO LONG AFTER THE WEDDING, I had to seek medical treatment. The exacerbation of my chronic illness is strongly affected by my emotional status. We went to the ER and I got admitted to a room. I remember the nurse asking my husband if he wanted a cot to stay with me. He said, "That wouldn't be necessary." The first day in the hospital, I usually am in a lot of pain and need someone to communicate for me. My husband wasn't there. He took the week off when I was in the hospital but he couldn't come to see me in the hospital until late in the afternoon. When I called and asked, "Where are you?" his response was that he was tired and needed to get some sleep.

I came home from the hospital barely able to walk and he asked me, "You are going to cook, right? Laundry hasn't been done since you were gone." I had to cook and do laundry while still sick. We didn't have much money, but I never thought he would not provide for me and protect me. It was painful to realize that he wasn't going to do those things.

Early in the marriage we had a blowout over a cell phone. I asked a question about a phone that we were trying to purchase. He began to scream at me. "Why didn't you wait for me? I thought we were going to do it together!" I went running into the bedroom and he kicked the door down. I took my keys and ran out the apartment. I called my friend and brothers in the church and told them what had happened. I was rattled and afraid that he had the potential to hurt me. I didn't understand how he could change from having a normal conversation to a man possessed. I tried to explain this flip, but no one understood what I was talking about. I felt that they thought I was exaggerating.

We had a physical altercation. I can't recall what it was about. He pushed me. I hit the couch hard and I sprang back up. I remember my wrist being gripped and remember limping the next day. I remember my coworkers asking me why I was limping and I said, "I tripped over something." I remember calling my girlfriend and she heard the sadness in my voice. She asked, "Did you talk to anyone?" I said I didn't feel comfortable talking to anyone, even my parents. I had to admit that, with all the other trials I had conquered in my life to survive, with all my health challenges, being in a marriage where someone physically harmed me was hard for me to swallow.

I remember coming home not knowing who I was facing. I would come home and stare at the apartment building in my car and prepare myself before I came in. As a Christian you are supposed to store up energy at home to go out into to the world. In my case, the opposite occurred. I stored up energy in the world to go home.

I wanted my relationship to work, so I kept changing to make it work, but he wasn't changing. The only thing that changed was what he said he needed. He would say, "I need space to deal with my emotions," and I would give him space. He would say, "No, I don't want to talk about it," or "You are always bothering me." I also stopped allowing family members to visit because I didn't think it was fair to expose them to what was happening at home.

After a fight he sometimes would come to me with apologies and flowers. But in most cases he behaved like nothing happened. When we met with other Christian couples to discuss our marital issues, he behaved like our fights never happened. I knew it happened but started to question my own thinking. I felt nervous. I actually started to believe that I must be crazy.

The more I wanted it to make sense of things, the more I felt controlled by his behaviors and my behaviors started not making sense. I had a lot of theories as to why he behaved the way he did. I began to think that something might have gone wrong while he was in the war. Because of this, I had to have more patience and give him more room. I was so into him that I lost me.

> Before marrying, I had peace even though I had a chronic illness. I had no money and was always looking for food, but was still joyful. I began to wonder, "How did I lose my joy?" None of the trials I faced in life had sucked the joy out of me. The scriptures state, "Don't let anyone steal your joy." In my marriage, I lost my joy and I lost me. I needed to fight to get me back and find my joy.

SUSAN

WE MARRIED SEVEN YEARS after we met—committed Christians, best friends. We loved God and each other. One August afternoon while attending the inaugural service for a new church planting three months into the marriage, I met a frightening, hostile stranger. He was my husband.

I was bewildered, dumbstruck. I spent the night in fear of him, thinking the marriage was over. Those eyes that had looked at me with such love, for some reason completely unknown to me suddenly seemed filled only with hate, contempt, and disgust. He refused to even speak to me, much less to tell me what had caused him such revulsion at the mere sight of me. I found myself apologizing, for what I didn't even know, but was nonetheless convinced I had inadvertently done something to offend him.

It was so long ago, I can't even remember the eventual outcome, but it was just the beginning of a scenario that would repeat itself over and over and over, growing more and more into a real life Dr. Jekyll and Mr. Hyde novel, with us as the main characters.

After more than six years with episodes growing in frequency with longer periods of emotional divorce in between the good times and the bad, God opened my eyes to the realization that I was not the cause. By then I had been so marginalized in my own thinking that I hardly recognized myself. Once a confident and capable woman, I had become tentative and unsure of myself. I had become so traumatized by my husband's unpredictable behavior that, although he had never physically assaulted me, I began to fear for my life.

The Church

The woman begins to recognize that the abuse has transformed her. She is no longer who she was, and this distresses her. She was once a joyful person, full of laughter; now she is not. She does not like the woman she has become but feels powerless to change. She comes to the church seeking clarity of her husband's behaviors and physical and emotional help.

DEBBIE

IT WAS EXHAUSTING to try to be someone you are not. I adapted in so many ways that it stole my joy. I begin to withdraw. I was always sad and my eyes were always on the verge of tears. I knew I once used to be this woman that loved to smile a lot, joke, and giggle. I couldn't find her; I didn't know where she lived. I wanted to find her, wanted to be her again, but she was so far away. I missed her.

At home, the abuse is intensifying. Everything is out of control. There is constant tension. She and the kids are constantly walking on eggshells. She has done everything she can to improve the relationship, but his abusive behaviors have not changed. He is becoming more unpredictable and his occasional gestures of kindness are getting shorter and less frequent, which decreases her opportunities for rest. She is physically and emotionally drained. Her thinking is overwhelmingly controlled by the relationship and by thoughts of leaving. Her fear of leaving, however, still is greater than the pain she feels in her relationship. She has fears of rejection or criticism from her family and the church if she does not make the marriage work. She fears that she will not be able to financially support herself and her children alone. She fears for her and her family's safety because he has threatened her with various dire consequences if she leaves. Regardless of all these fears, she wants the marriage to work. She thinks that if he seeks help and changes, the marriage will be saved.

In church, she is quiet, hoping that someone will ask, "What is wrong? How is your marriage?" She thinks, "Maybe they will see I am unhappy and sad. Maybe they will see his deceptive behaviors and challenge him." No one, however, asks, or, if she gives a hint about what is going on, probes deeper. No one sees past his deception.

NANCY

IT WAS EXTREMELY HARD to be open about what was happening. I would leave hints here and there or talk a little about a piece of it. I would try and let the bruises be visible, hoping someone would care enough to ask and that I would be brave enough to answer. I had a very difficult time being direct or ever getting to the part of what happened when things got really bad. I wanted to believe that everything would be OK and would often get advice about how I should be a better wife or work on myself and repent.

During the church services, she listens intently, especially when the sermon is about relationships, hoping to hear the word "domestic violence" or "abuse." Domestic violence is never mentioned. Instead, what she hears creates spiritual conflicts. For example, scriptures like 1 Peter 3:5 give the example of how holy women of the past submitted to their husbands. "What is meant by 'submission'?" she asks. Does it mean having no input in the decision making process and doing everything he tells her to do? Does it mean she stands still while he calls her degrading and belittling names in the presence of her kids and family? Does it mean being a "door mat"? When she accepts his abusive behavior, is she confirming that this behavior is OK? She also struggles with 1 Peter 3:1, which states, "Submit to your husbands, so that if any one of them does not believe, they may be won over." Her interpretation of this scripture influences the belief that her submission will change her husband or, if he is not a Christian, will lead to his conversion. She takes responsibility for her husband's salvation.

When he does not change, she begins to doubt her own faith. Does she have enough faith? If she does, why is he not changing his abusive behaviors toward her? Is it because she is in sin? Are her sins hindering God from changing him? Are there hidden sins that need to be forgiven? She struggles with these questions. She wonders, "Why is this happening to me? I have done everything God asks, why is my husband not changing? Where are you, God?"

The sermon provokes conflicting emotions but does not answer her questions. It does not clearly define the meaning and limits of submission as described in the Bible. She leaves church feeling guilty and confused.

When she goes for advice, she is told that her husband is the head of the house. If she has problems submitting to him, she has problems submitting to God, because her relationship with her husband is a reflection of her relationship with God. Will she ever have a good relationship with God, since her relationship with her husband is cool, distant, and distrustful? She is told that God hates divorce (Malachi 2:16) and that the family needs to stay together. If she chooses to divorce, she cannot remarry.

Sarah and Abigail are used as examples of submission. Sarah called her husband her master (1 Peter 3:6). In 1 Samuel 25, Abigail's husband was harsh and mean, yet she stood by him. The abused woman is encouraged to imitate Sarah and Abigail in being submissive.

As she opens up about what is has happening at home, her forgiveness is questioned. People in the church ask, "Why are you angry? Didn't you forgive him?" She hears statements like, "You just need to forgive him and move on," or "You both are in sin and need to repent." Didn't Jesus say in Matthew 18:21–22 "to forgive seventy times seven"? She asks herself, "If I have forgiven him, why do I react to his behaviors? Why does he provoke the same emotions as before?"

No one uses Jesus' teachings in Matthew 18:15–17 which teach that forgiveness is a process. Forgiveness requires justice and accountability. No one talks about premature forgiveness as denial.[2] She is told to forgive, even though he has not repented or admitted his responsibility.

DEBBIE

I WENT LOOKING FOR HELP within the church. I wanted someone to validate what was going on. I was looking to hear what he was doing was wrong. Before any meeting with people in the church, he would say, "We are not going to share, this and that, right?" The backlash I expected to receive determined what I was willing to share. During the sessions it felt like I was hearing the same conversation. If I asked, "Why did this happen?" the same question would be directed at me. The responsibility always came back to me. I wasn't doing the right thing. I always needed to forgive and repent. I was always the one who needed to change. I know I had my faults and sins. I knew that, but I was crying for help. I would take the advice and try to change. I had to forgive. I had to be like godly women in the scriptures. I had to be humble and do what my husband said. When he told me I was mean or lazy, I had to believe that and work up the energy to be friendlier or more energetic and fight to get stuff done at home.

He got a slap on the hand and his issues were not addressed. There was no accountability on his part. What about repentance? I barely got the acknowledgement that his behaviors were wrong. New things were revealed but there always was an excuse and no responsibility on his part or change in his behaviors. I was nagging when I requested an explanation for bounced rent checks, pornography, no money in the account with no truthful explanation, or his coming home at 2:00 or 3:00 in the morning. There was no acknowledgement of the problem. I was expected to turn off the switch and not talk about these issues again.

I believe forgiveness was used in a manner never intended by the Bible. Once he said, "I am sorry," I was automatically expected to forgive him regardless of whether his behavior changed or not. At times it appeared that he had changed, but he just switched to a different bad behavior.

She begins to question God's justice. She wonders, "Why am I suffering for no reason?" She hears comments such as, "You made your bed;

now you must lie in it." She is told that the abuse is her cross to bear and that she should persevere in her sufferings. Didn't Jesus do that on the way to the cross? On the way to the cross, as recounted in 1 Peter 2:21–23, the crowd hurled insults, hit, and spat on Jesus but he did not retaliate. She also should bear her cross in silence—like Jesus.

In desperation, she convinces her husband to obtain couples' counseling within the church. But in couples' counseling, she does not tell the whole story of her abuse because it is humiliating and confusing. She hopes that when her husband tells his side of the story, the church counselor will see the inconsistency and rebuke him. But his version of events is smooth, with details about events and dates. He is in control. She ends up defending herself because his version is full of accusations toward her. As she tries to defend herself, she appears emotional and irrational. Counseling becomes an extension of the abuse that is happening at home.

The more she opens up in church, the more her scared self is exposed, which creates shame and humiliation. She begins to feel people are talking about her, making it difficult to worship God and leading to emotional isolation. The scriptures also become a source of turmoil. Instead of gaining clarity from the scriptures, she becomes more confused. This confusion affects her relationship with God. God should be the source of peace; instead, she makes him the source of conflict.

DEBBIE

I HAD TO RECONCILE with God. The final fight was between God and me. I was no longer going to allow my husband to provoke me. I was going to behave toward him from a place centered in love. If it was not centered in love, I was not going to speak. That was my first conviction. I refused to fight. He was going to pick a fight on his own. I refused to fuel his behavior. When he tried to make me angry, I could see it. I took three days alone with me and my Bible, thesaurus, and audio Bible for times when I didn't have the energy to read. I decided I couldn't be good with anybody if I was not good with God. This was my first fight with God. I had to kill the toxicity. I wasn't going have anger control my emotions. My strength started to return and peace started to return.

No one could help me to survive except God. No one could fuel me but him. I was in pure survival mode. It was life and death. I knew that I couldn't exist without God if I was not completely whole with him. If I was whole, I could get through anything. I had been sick multiple times and on my deathbed, the doctor told my family that I wasn't going to make it, but I did. If God could pull me through those events, I knew he was able to pull me through this marriage. I knew if I didn't work it out I was going to die. I didn't know how I was going to die, but I knew the mental starvation that I was experiencing in my relationship had the potential to kill me physically and spiritually. If I didn't get rest I was going to die. I needed to do something. I had to make a change to survive.

I was not going to fight and I still had to be respectful. I became conscious of the stories I told people about him because he still is a person. Everyone has his or her struggles; it was not fair to blast it out for everyone to hear. I tried to be respectful and conscious of how I was interacting with him. I wanted a clear conscience with God and nothing my husband could hold against me. If he made anything up it was fine, because my conscience was clear.

CHAPTER 2

DYNAMICS OF DOMESTIC VIOLENCE

The abused woman and those who are willing to help must educate themselves about domestic violence. Education provides an understanding of how violence negatively impacts the abused woman's physical and mental wellbeing. Education is the first step toward empowerment.

According to the World Health Organization, intimate partner violence or domestic violence is "...behavior in an intimate relationship that causes physical, sexual or psychological harm, including sexual coercion, psychological abuse, and controlling behaviors."[1] Many people assume that abuse produces obvious physical signs, such as a black eye, broken bones, etc.

Instead of being physical, abuse can be less noticeable, as in the case of psychological emotional abuse.[2] Although abusers vary in the tactics they use, they share the common goal of establishing and maintaining control over their relationships. Below are lists of common behaviors of an abuser. Most abusers will exhibit some, but not all of these behaviors.

Tactics the Abuser Uses to Achieve and Maintain Control

Emotional or Psychological Abuse

Emotional or psychological abuse involves the "... use of voice, action. The danger of this type of abuse is it that the abuser is shrewd and his motives are deceptive, making it difficult for the victim to prove. Most victims will agree that psychological abuse is more damaging or equal to physical abuse. Since there are no physical signs of abuse, it comes down to the victim's word against the abuser."[3] Types of emotional and psychological abuse include the following:[3,4]

Verbal Abuse
- Constant criticism
- Mocking
- Name-calling like, "stupid," "bitch," "whore," and "crazy"
- Insulting remarks like "you never do anything right," "you're a worthless mother"
- Yelling and swearing
- Threats to use violence
- Accusations of unfaithfulness
- Demeaning jokes
- Sarcasm

Isolation
- Making it hard for the woman to see her friends and relatives or to participate in activities that are important to her
- Sabotaging the woman's relationship with her children, other family members, and friends
- Relocating so that the woman loses her support system
- Making accusations against her friends or family
- Monitoring the woman's phone calls
- Controlling where she goes
- Taking the woman's car keys
- Destroying her important documents, such as passport or immigration papers

Coercion
- Constantly causing the woman to feel guilty
- Always insisting on being right
- Making up impossible rules and punishing the woman for breaking them
- Threatening self-harm or suicide
- Deliberately doing things that will cause trouble or embarrassment for the woman and her family

Harassment
- Following or stalking the woman
- Embarrassing her in public
- Refusing to leave when asked
- Constantly checking up on the woman, including calling her constantly when she is not with him, or checking her computer activity
- Reading her correspondence (mail, e-mails, texts, tracking her online)

Abusing trust
- Frequent lying
- Unreliability, constant breaking of promises
- Withholding important information, such the family's financial status
- Extramarital affairs, intentionally promiscuous behavior (e.g., flirts in front of her, coming on to her friends and family members)
- Extreme jealousy and possessiveness
- Refusing to share domestic responsibilities

Threats and intimidation
- Threatening to harm the woman and/or her children, pets, family, and friends
- Using physical size to intimidate
- Keeping weapons and threatening to use them
- Destroying partner's or children's possessions
- Punching walls or doors; throwing, kicking, breaking objects in "anger" (door, car, furniture)
- Clenching fist as a threat
- Driving recklessly with the woman and children in the vehicle

Emotional withholding
- Emotional distance, coldness
- Withholding compliments

- Silent treatment
- Disregarding or downplaying the woman's feelings, concerns, and opinions when she expresses them

Physical Abuse (involves not only physical contact but also using objects or presence) [5,6]
- Hitting
- Slapping
- Kicking
- Choking
- Pushing
- Punching
- Beating
- Arm twisting
- Hair pulling
- Banging head against wall or floor
- Sitting or standing on partner
- Physically blocking her movement (e.g., standing in the doorway)
- Locking partner out of the house
- Throwing objects at the woman, children, pets, etc.

Sexual Abuse

In an abusive relationship, the man may use sex as a means to exert power to shame and humiliate his wife. Many women are very hesitant to admit this type of abuse.[5] Examples of sexual abuse toward a partner include:
- Forcing sex on a woman (this is rape, whether it occurs between married or unmarried partners)
- Demanding sexual acts that the woman does not want to perform
- Engaging in sex after violence
- Engaging in sex when the woman is physically exhausted or ill
- Unwanted touching
- Rough and/or painful sex
- Withholding sex as a punishment

Economic Abuse [3, 4]
- Not paying bills
- Refusing to give the woman money
- Not allowing the woman to work or obtain further training/education
- Interfering with/jeopardizing the woman's job
- Refusing to work and support the family

Spiritual Abuse [6]

Spiritual abuse uses religious beliefs, teachings, and traditions to support physical, psychological, and sexual abuse. This abuse is damaging to a Christian woman and her children because it jeopardizes their relationship with God. The abuser may profess to be a Christian or may never have set foot in a church but still uses religion to justify the abuse. Examples of spiritual abuse include the following:

- Denying or discrediting her spiritual values as unimportant or foolish
- Using religion to justify his position as controller
- Preventing her from going to church
- Using religion to instill fear and coerce (e.g., "If you don't do as I say, you'll go to hell.")
- Defiling or destroying books and other religious materials that are meaningful to the woman
- Inappropriate use of "male privilege—duty to obey"

Power and Control Wheel

The Power and Control Wheel was developed through the Domestic Abuse Intervention Project in Duluth, Minnesota, as a visual representation of the types of abusive behaviors or tactics used by the abuser. In the middle of the wheel is his motivation for the abuse, which always is to establish and maintain power and control.

The outer rim of the wheel represents physical and sexual violence. Physical and sexual abuse is used periodically to maintain the control that is continually being reinforced by the behaviors inside the wheel.[7]

202 East Superior Street Duluth, MN 55802
218-722-2781
www.theduluthmodel.org

"The Cycle of Violence" (as developed by Lenore Walker)

In her book *The Battered Woman*, Lenore E. Walker presents interviews with victims of domestic violence relationships; she notes three distinct phases: (1) tension-building, (2) acute battering, and (3) honeymoon phase.[8]

Tension-building phase. Tension builds up in the relationship due to minor abusive incidents. He becomes more critical, angry, jealous, and suspicious of her behaviors. He increases name-calling, verbal threats, and intimidation; or he becomes cold, distant, and withdrawn. She knows that there is going to be an explosion of violent behaviors but does not know when. The woman "walks on eggshells" to keep the violence from escalating by trying to keep everything calm and/or doing what the abuser wants. Or, she may withdraw and stay away from him. When she withdraws, he may become more hostile and try to provoke her to get angry, using her reaction to justify his abusive behaviors.

As the tension increases, the woman realizes that her strategies for controlling the situation are not working, and she experiences increasing fear and anxiety. Her body prepares for the impending doom by inciting the "fight or flight" response. Her heart rate increases, her stomach feels queasy, her muscles become tense, and her senses are heightened.

She may physically fight back or may feel powerless to fight or run. At times it is easier to provoke the violence in order to shorten the tension phase so that she can minimize the psychological and physiological torture she is experiencing and move on to the honeymoon phase. There is no set time frame for how long this phase lasts. It could last for days, weeks, months, or even years.

Serious battering phase. In this second phase, the woman no longer is able to avoid the violence because the abuser stops trying to control his aggressive behaviors. This phase is characterized by violent episodes that may include physical assault, sexual abuse, or extreme emotional abuse. This phase may last for several hours or days.

When the acute attack is over and there are visible signs of the abuse, the woman may feel humiliated and embarrassed to let others see her bruises. She may attempt to cover her marks or may isolate herself from others. She may minimize her injuries and may not seek medical help until several days later. By not exposing or reporting her injuries, she is able to deny or to pretend that the abuse did not happen.

During this phase, she may be in a state of shock and experience listlessness, depression, and a feeling of helplessness. She does not understand the reason for the violence. In this phase, she might contemplate leaving the relationship but has no detailed plan for doing so. Since she has no well thought-out plan for leaving, her abuser easily lures the woman into the honeymoon phase and thoughts about leaving diminish.

Honeymoon phase. "The honeymoon phase comprises unreliable intervals of kindness and apologetic behaviors on the part of the abuser."[9] The abuser apologizes for his abusive behaviors and promises not to repeat them. He may state that he is going to seek help or agree to go for counseling. When the physical violence is obvious (e.g., bruises), the honeymoon phase may be more defined because the abuser does not want the woman to seek legal assistance or expose him to others.

The woman believes that if he seeks counseling, he will stop his abusive behaviors. In this phase, the abuser may become very affectionate and give her flowers, candy, and expensive gifts. He may cook, clean the house, take care of the kids, and take her to dinner. All these behaviors reinforce the idea that he can change and become non-abusive. She begins to fantasize that the relationship will become the kind of relationship she has hoped for. This hope causes her to convince herself that "it wasn't that bad."

Over time, the honeymoon phase may become less effective. The woman may feel pressured or manipulated into accepting the abuser's presents or gestures of kindness. In the past, he may have taken the presents away or destroyed them during an angry outburst. As a result, the woman has no emotional attachment to his gifts. She may, however, be afraid to refuse the presents and/or afraid not to be receptive to his "kind" behaviors because if she does, the tension and abusive cycles resume.

In this phase, the woman also can feel controlled and confused, because she is not ready to forgive and the reasons for the violence are still not clear to her. She may feel trapped, guilty, and forced to move past her anger over the abuse because of his smothering gestures of kindness.

Not every woman experiences "the cycle of violence" sequence or is aware that she is in the cycle of violence, especially when there is no physical assault. Some women's experiences are more random, infrequent, or unpredictable.[10] She may experience the tension-building and the battering phases in a single day. When the woman begins to expose the abuse or begins to take control of her life, the honeymoon phase may become less frequent or not occur at all.

In relationships where there is no physical assault, women may not believe that they are being abused.[11] "Abuse almost always escalates if there is no intervention. Once physical violence enters a relationship, it gets worse, not better."[12] It is important to remember that "with each escalating cycle, the abuse becomes more severe, and the respite or break period where no abuse is occurring diminishes or disappears".[13]

Impact of Abuse on the Woman

Domestic violence, whether physical, sexual, or psychological, can lead to psychological consequences for the victims.[14] Studies provide convincing evidence that the effects of exposure to violence are not temporary but may endure for many years. The more severe the abuse, the greater its impact on the victim's physical and mental health.[15]

Symptoms of PTSD. Common psychological effects of violence on the abused woman may include flashbacks, intrusive imagery, nightmares, anxiety, emotional numbing, insomnia (difficulty sleeping), hyper-vigilance, and avoidance of traumatic triggers.[16] A woman experiencing PTSD may have difficulty sleeping and be unable to focus on her daily life. She may be consumed by thoughts and memories of the abuse or by figuring out ways to avoid the abuse.

Paralyzing fear. The woman lives in constant fear of violence. Her fear consumes her day-to-day life and destroys her ability to recognize and think through the choices she has to seek change.

Shame, humiliation. The woman may live in constant shame because of her situation. Over time she may isolate herself because of her shame. She also feels shame because her abuser constantly humiliates her. He may succeed in making her feel that she deserves the abuse.

Low self-esteem/insecurity. The woman's sense of self-worth is low, partly because of her sense of shame and constant humiliation. As a result, she may underestimate her abilities and feel incapable of making changes. As her self-esteem decreases, she may find that her ability to perform in every area of life decreases.

Guilt. Over time the woman increasingly accepts blame for family problems. The abuser works hard to convince her that she is responsible for his abusive behaviors and makes her a scapegoat for problems he creates. She increasingly feels responsible for his actions and may blame herself for not being able to change his abusive behaviors.

Helplessness or hopelessness. The woman comes to believe that she has no control over her situation. She may become submissive and accept the violence as she loses her sense of personal power. Continual disappointments also lead her to lose hope because nothing she does seems to change her situation.[17] Over time, her sense of helplessness and lack of hope negatively affect her ability to make decisions and take action to change her situation.

Hopes for change in the marriage—"Fantasy of Change." The abused woman may retain hope, but it is a false hope or a "fantasy of change" in her relationship. She hopes that someday the violence will stop and her marriage will become a normal, happy relationship. This hope keeps many abuse victims, especially Christian women, in abusive relationships.[18]

Fatigue. The abused woman is overwhelmed by the abuse and becomes emotionally and physically drained. She may be so tired that she is unable to feel or react to the abuse.

Emotional numbness. A woman may find that her emotional responses are duller than before and that she often feels numb. This emotional numbness reduces the pain she experiences and allows her to endure the abuse.

Suppressed anger. The abused woman naturally experiences anger about her abuse. Fears of her abuser as well as her shame often keep her from directly expressing this anger. She therefore suppresses the anger, which may manifest as irritability, fits of rage directed at other targets, depression, and illness.

Depression. The most common psychological response to abuse. Sixty percent of battered women report symptoms of depression.[19]

Denial: The Glue That Binds

Some behaviors that a woman develops in response to the abuse are coping strategies. Pamela Cooper-White, in *Women Healing and Empowering*, notes that a "…powerful force in abusive relationships is denial." Denial allows the abused woman to protect her mind from painful realities. Denial allows the woman to convince herself that the abuse did not happen or that the abuse is not as bad as it actually is. When the woman overuses denial in a situation of repeated harm, she places herself in greater danger because she is turning off her body's natural warning system.[20] The woman also may deny her own emotions: for example, that she is angry about being unjustly abused.[21] As a result of her denial, the woman may become trapped in an abusive relationship for a very long time. Types of denial, according to Pamela Cooper-White, include the following:

Minimizing. Believing that what has happened to her was not really so bad. For example, the woman is seen in the emergency room with a broken jaw. She might say, "It was just a little family disagreement."

Forgetting. Consciously or unconsciously re-working the abusive event in to her mind until she convinces herself that things were not so bad. She forgets the details of what happened and pushes them out of her mind or forgets the intensity of her emotions at the time of the incident. After a severe beating resulting in bruises and other injuries, she might say, "I wasn't really afraid because I knew he wouldn't kill me."

Premature forgiving. Forgiving her abuser, putting the past behind her and moving on to what she hopes will be an abuse-free future. The woman believes that her partner will not abuse her again, a belief that is reinforced by the "honeymoon" phase.

Making excuses for the abuser. Minimizing the abuser's responsibility. For example, the woman may say "He was under a lot of stress," or, "He was drinking too much, and things got out of hand."

Normalizing. Viewing the abusive behavior as normal. The woman may say, "Every family has their bad moments," or, "This kind of thing happens in every family, and it is just a part of life."

Exceptionalizing. Viewing the abusive incident as completely unusual and overlooking it. The woman may say, "He was under so much stress. This won't happen again."

The woman must end the pattern of denial. When she does this, she will able to break free from the glue that binds her to the abusive relationship.

Reasons Why She Stays

The abused woman often is judged by others who make statements like, "Why can't you leave the relationship?" Leaving is not as simple as others may think. There are legitimate reasons behind the woman's decision to stay in an abusive relationship. Some of these reasons are as follows:

Love. A Harris Interactive online survey of 2,500 females, ages 18 to 35, who reported experiencing abuse, found that the number one reason why these women stayed in an abusive relationship was love.[22] The woman probably fell in love with her abuser at some point, and he demonstrated positive qualities and loving behavior when he was not abusive. The honeymoon phase continues to reinforce those positive qualities.

Parenting. She wants the children to have a father. She has an ideal of a "normal" father who is involved in the lives of the children. Some abusive partners actually are good fathers, which give the abused woman an incentive to stay.

Hope for change. She has hope that he can change. She believes it is possible that the violence will stop, she will have a normal family life, and her children will grow up in a nurturing two-parent family. Women may initially have this hope because they are taught to believe in those they care about, particularly if they are religious or spiritual. As the abuse continues, her hope becomes a fantasy that keeps her bound to the relationship.

Denial. Everyone uses certain forms of denial as a coping mechanism on occasion. As described in the earlier section, this coping strategy is a typical response to abuse that, when overused, can keep the woman in the abusive relationship.

Fears. The abused woman has many legitimate fears that hinder her from leaving her abuser. These include:

- *Fear for her own safety.* The woman faces real physical danger when she attempts to leave an abusive relationship. Over 75 percent of domestic homicides occur when a woman attempts to leave or has left her abuser.[23] In many cases, attempts to leave will be accompanied by increased violence, threats, and other extreme actions by the abuser to stop the woman from leaving.
- *Fear for her children.* The two major reasons that victims of abuse give for both staying with and leaving their abusive partners are the safety and welfare of their children.[25] The woman fears for the safety and welfare of her children because the abuser threatens to harm her if she leaves. She also may

fear losing custody of her children or fear that he will kidnap them. In addition, she may fear that she will not be able to both physically and financially care for the children by herself, particularly if she has limited resources and social support.
- *Fear of not having a partner.* In our society, there is strong social pressure to have a partner. A woman may feel that she is not complete without a partner.
- *Fear of being cut off from her community.* A woman may fear rejection from her family members, community, and/or church if she leaves her partner.
- *Fear of financial insecurity.* A woman may fear losing her financial and material assets if she leaves her abuser. She may face losing her home, her savings/investments, and other assets that she has worked for and which provide security for her and her family.

Financial dependence on the abuser. An abused woman often will have little or no money because her partner controls all the finances and is secretive about their financial status. She may not be able to access the money by herself and/or her partner might leave her with financial debt that eliminates resources she would need to survive on her own. In addition, a woman who has been a homemaker for many years will have great difficulty finding employment that allows her to adequately support herself and her children.

Lack of support/resources. An abused woman often is isolated from her social support system. She may have lost connections to family, friends, church, and other supportive groups, due to constant moves and/or threats and misbehavior on the part of the abuser. She also may be unaware of resources in the community because of her isolation and other abusive and controlling behaviors by her partner. For example, a woman who is not allowed to continue her education may have greater difficulty accessing information that she needs, though a woman of any level of education may lack knowledge about domestic violence and related resources.

Religious beliefs/scriptures. Many cultures and religions teach that marriage is for "better or worse" and "till death do us part." Many religions strongly discourage or prohibit divorce and the breakup of the family unit. A woman may be called to forgive and return to her abuser. She may be taught that God will punish her if she seeks to end her marriage.

Shame. As noted earlier, the woman normally is ashamed of her abuse and does not feel comfortable exposing it. Leaving her partner normally requires that she expose the abuse.

Conclusion

When the woman, and those who are willing to help her understand the dynamic of domestic violence, she is better equipped to make the necessary steps to break free from the effects of the violence. The woman and the community must also gain awareness of the resources in the community that will allow her to effectively seek change.

CHAPTER 3

SPIRITUAL DILEMMAS

When experiencing abuse at home, the Christian woman comes to the church seeking help and clarity. The advice given, however, may lead to more confusion. This confusion affects the woman's relationship with God and leads to spiritual dilemmas. Spiritual dilemmas relate to abandonment by God, the nature for suffering, the value of obedience, and biblical justification for separation and divorce.[1]

This chapter addresses each of these areas of spiritual dilemma. It is designed to help the abused woman address misconceptions about the scriptures as she tries to understand what is happening to her. In addition to covering many passages that cause spiritual dilemmas for abused Christian women, stories from Christian women are included describing their struggles with understanding these verses and the experts' interpretations.

 **EDITH**

LORD, I FIND IT DIFFICULT to tell my story. Sometimes I forget the details. I forget the conflict. I forget the emotions because you have helped me to overcome. If it is your will, help me to recall as if it was yesterday.

I remember searching for you because I felt lonely and needed your peace. I needed your peace in my time of storm. My life was a storm then. My marriage had fallen apart and the abuse had intensified. In my mind, I felt like I was locked in prison. Instead of loving me, my husband made me fear him. Yet you made me feel like I was in the eye of the storm—all around me was chaos, but you kept me in a place of peace and calmness. You, Lord, were like the light that brightens the ground after a storm. The peace and beauty you showed me motivated me to wake up at 4:00 a.m. to worship you. I was eager to meditate in your Word because I knew that in you alone I would find my strength and peace.

Although I had your peace, I still found myself wanting answers from you. I remember struggling and wrestling with you. I remember asking the "why" questions. I remember questioning my faith. If I had faith, then why wasn't my husband changing? I remember being told that my relationship with my husband is the same as my relationship with God. WOW! Will I ever have a good relationship with you since my relationship with my husband is cool and distant? I remember asking the questions about forgiveness. Does it mean I haven't forgiven my husband because I react to his behaviors? If I have forgiven, why does he provoke the same emotions as before?

What about suffering? We are supposed to persevere in our sufferings. I remember someone using 1 Peter 2 to demonstrate that I must persevere in my sufferings. Is my relationship to my husband the same as a slave to his master? I am commanded to respect my husband, but am I a slave? Am I a slave to be beaten by my master? Sarah called her husband "master," but Abraham loved his wife and always protected her. If he is my master, as Abraham was Sarah's, he should protect and not hurt me.

What about the instructions to submit? Was I submissive enough? Does submission mean that I do not have any input in the decision-making process and must do everything he tells me to do? Does it mean I stand still while he screams at me with degrading and belittling names in the presence of my children? Doesn't that tell him and my children that it is OK for someone to call someone else stupid or degrading names? What a dilemma!

I constantly felt guilty, fearful, anxious, angry, shameful, hopeless, and helpless. I felt guilty because I thought about giving up on my marriage. Does

> it mean that I am impatient to wait for change? Did that mean I didn't trust you to change my situation?
>
> But during my times of confusion, you were there. You showed me that the solution was to separate and escape the abuse. I struggled with this solution because I did not want to break my marriage covenant and my understanding of your scriptures. I wanted my reasons to leave to be based on biblical convictions. I examined scriptures that dealt with marriage and divorce and found that adultery was a reason for divorce (Matthew 19:9). My husband committed adultery, but I forgave him for that. I thought about leaving after a bad beating, and had him arrested, but ended up taking him back. Ultimately, I developed a personal conviction and left my marriage because of the psychological and physical abuse. No one deserves to be beaten down physically and emotionally, especially by a person who professes to love her. In Malachi 2:16, you said you hate divorce but you also "hate a man's covering himself with violence." When I accepted Christ as my Lord, you gave me the same inheritance as every other Christian. You love me same as everyone else in your family. You love me and don't want me to be abused.

Abandonment by God

Her husband has successfully isolated her from her family and close friends. She also feels alienated from the church. She thinks people are whispering about her in the pews or social events as she walks by; as a result, she withdraws and isolates herself. To complicate her situation, some of her friends are tired of hearing her story and they believe she is not speaking the truth about what is going on at home. They stop listening to her story or pretend to listen, but non-verbal clues indicate that they are not paying attention. She feels ignored when in their presence and begins to experience intense feelings of isolation and loneliness. With no support system, she feels helpless.

In her book, *Keeping the Faith*, Marie Fortune says that "some people may turn away from a woman experiencing abuse just when she needs them the most because they do not understand what she is going through. It may frighten them and make them uncomfortable, so they blame the victim for having been abused. They may believe that if they avoid contact with the victim they will somehow protect themselves from the same kind of pain and suffering. Their avoidance increases the woman's isolation and makes her feel even worse about herself."[2]

Feeling alone, the abused woman turns to God for comfort. But she is not fully able to receive his comfort because she is struggling to understand why he is allowing the abuse to happen to her. She is a good Christian wife and has been praying hard for her husband to change, but God is not answering her prayers. She asks, "Where is God?" Why has he forsaken her? Is God punishing her for her sins by abandoning her?"

DEBBIE

YOU GET MAD AT YOURSELF for letting it happen. But you believe that is what you are supposed to do. I went into my marriage knowing that we would never part until death. I remember feeling abandoned by God. I prayed for the relationship from the beginning of the courtship and all the way into the marriage. Every single step of the way I would ask God, "Is this the right thing?" Lead me to what I am supposed to do. I want to be a good wife and I want to have a good husband.

The reality is that God has not forsaken her and will be with her even when it seems that everyone else has abandoned her. God is always with her, surrounding her with his love, and showering her with strength and courage to free herself. He has been giving her clues or answers to her questions, but she may not have been ready for his answers. She has been wrapped up in the abuse and how to fix the relationship, so that it has consumed her thinking to the point where she has lost touch with God's presence. She took her focus away from God and placed it on her husband.

Her relationship with God has to be the highest priority, before her relationship with her husband. God is waiting for her to turn to him and he is saying to her, "I can help you but you have to let me. It may be hard for you to do what is needed, but I am going to be with you all the way." He has given her the power to choose the right thing by giving her a conscience. As a Christian, she also has, in addition to the scriptures, the power of the Holy Spirit within her to help her make decisions.

The scriptures have numerous examples of oppressed people crying out to God for deliverance. Job lamenting in his sackcloth and ashes, the helpless, orphans, those who have been treated unjustly all cried out to God. God heard their prayers, and he will hear her prayers today and will deliver her from her abuse. In 2 Samuel 22:3-4, David says, "My God is my rock, in whom I find protection. He is my shield, the strength of my salvation, and my stronghold, my high tower, my savior, the one who saves me from violence." Psalms 10:17, 12:5, 103:6, and 140 all reassure her that he wants to deliver her from her oppressors. The fact that God will deliver her from her violence, however, is not a reason to continue to accept the violence until God miraculously rescues her.

DEBBIE

I WAS SUPPOSED TO LET GOD vindicate me. I kept waiting for God to vindicate me. I cried out "God please vindicate me!" He knew my motives were pure. He knew that I had been praying all the way though my marriage. I relied on him to make the changes I made. I honestly believed those changes would give me the results I wanted. My heart never left him. I was angry at times but my heart never left God. I tried to hide from God. I would tell myself I am not going to read the Bible any more, but this only lasted three days because the Word of God was my life. I couldn't do without it. It kept me alive; sustained me. My faith sustained me. I believe in God's love and felt it. That was the only reason that I am alive today. I had to say to myself, "God has given you the power to vindicate yourself; you don't need that vindication from others. He has given it to you. Pick up your sleeping mat and walk!"

The Nature of Suffering

She is told to pray for the happiness of those who curse and hurt her, including her husband. She also is told that if someone slaps her on one cheek, to turn the other cheek (Matthew 5:39–40). She also is reminded of Luke 6:27–29, where Jesus states, "But if you are willing to listen, I say, love your enemies. Do well to those who hate you." She sees that 1 Peter 2:21–23 states, "To this you were called, because Christ suffered for you, leaving you an example, that you should follow his steps. He committed no sin, and no deceit was found in his mouth. When they hurled their insults at him, he did not retaliate. When he suffered, he made no threats. Instead, he entrusted himself to him who judges justly." Didn't Christ suffer unjustly? Doesn't this mean that it is Christlike to suffer this way? She is told to follow his footsteps. She needs to recognize that Christ went voluntarily to the cross. His suffering was for a greater good, salvation for all.

Her suffering is involuntary and has no benefit to anyone, not even her husband. She must consider whether she is doing the right thing by continuing to accept violence. How is his abuse justified? What are the good results from the abuse? Is standing and letting him inflict pain voluntary suffering? Did she choose to be beaten or verbally abused? Does her unjustified suffering convert her husband?

Marie Fortune states, "The suffering from being battered physically and psychologically is involuntary. It is put upon you against your will. You never choose it. It has no good purpose. It is not God's will for your life. To accept it as purposeful, as your cross to bear, as God's will for you, is to allow yourself to be a victim."[3]

She is told that her marriage is her "cross to bear." Is it her "cross" to be brutally beaten until she has black eyes and swollen lips? Is this violent act her "cross"? Does bearing her cross mean she accepts verbal insults, threats of physical harm, or isolation from her support system? Is emotional abuse her cross?

Jesus said, "If any of you wants to be my follower, you must turn from your selfish ways, take up your cross, and follow me" (Matthew 16:24, NLT) and, "You cannot be my disciple if you do not carry your own cross, and follow me" (Luke 14:27, NLT). What does this mean?

Denying herself means letting Christ lead her and surrendering to him before her husband. Surrendering to God's will does not mean accepting senseless abuse and the abuser's lack of repentance. Carrying her cross does not mean accepting every mistreatment by others, especially when God has given her the power to seek change. Too often, Christian friends respond to her abuse by simply advising her to pray harder for her husband because God can change her situation—by which they mean, go back and take the abuse because it is God's will for her present life. Covering up someone else's sins and quietly accepting abuse is not the kind of suffering that leads to good results. It is not God's will for her life.

Jesus came to free her from captivity and oppression (Luke 4:18–19) and to bind and comfort her broken heart (Isaiah 61:1–2). This means that he came to free her from her abuser and comfort her during her times of suffering. Since he has set her free, she needs to no longer be burdened by the bondage of abuse (Galatians 5:1). He wants her to live life to the fullest (John 10:10), which means a life free of violence for her children and herself.

When Jesus was crucified, he took upon himself the suffering deserved by all sinners. Therefore, she doesn't have to suffer as he did. 1 Peter 2:24 states, "He personally carried away our sins in his own body on the cross. So we can be dead to sins and live for what is right."

NANCY

I HAD FOUND OUT he had cheated on me during that first year of marriage and that I was pregnant again; but I wanted so much to be like Jesus, so I forgave him and the abuse. I thought surely things would be different now that Jesus "would fix it." The first month of being Christians, we had a fight and I wanted to leave. He was supposed to let me leave but he kicked the keys out of my hand and broke my finger. He said it wasn't broken and that I should not have an X-ray because I was pregnant. A member of my church encouraged us to

> get it checked. He was mad but came from work to meet me at the Urgent Care. I was pregnant and carrying the other baby in the car seat. He stayed by my side and I felt like he loved me. As I suspected, it was broken, it was splinted and I was referred to the orthopedic surgeon. I told the surgeon that my husband knew karate and tried to make it a joke. I felt encouraged to make light of it and to "lie" to everyone about what happened, so I continued to make jokes about it or make light of it. I was very good at covering the abuse.

The Value of Obedience

The following scriptures create a significant dilemma for the abused Christian woman seeking help from her church:

> Wives, in the same way be submissive to your husbands so that, if any of them do not believe the word, they may be won over without words by the behavior of their wives, when they see the purity and reverence of your lives. Your beauty should not come from outward adornment, such as braided hair and the wearing of gold jewelry and fine clothes. Instead, it should be that of your inner self, the unfading beauty of a gentle and quiet spirit, which is of great worth in God's sight. (1 Peter 3:1–4, NIV)

> Wives, submit to your husbands as to the Lord. For the husband is the head of the wife as Christ is the head of the church, his body, of which he is the Savior. Now as the church submits to Christ, so also wives should submit to their husbands in everything. (Ephesians 5:22–24, NIV)

She is taught that the husband is the head of his wife as Christ is the head of the church. She is to submit to him as the church submits to Christ in "everything." Her relationship to her husband is directly related to her relationship with God. Her role is to honor and respect her husband. When she is submissive to him she is honoring his lordship. The non-Christian husband can be won over to Christ by the behaviors of his wife. She may believe, therefore, that she should silently accept abuse from her husband.

>  **DEBBIE**
>
> **I HAD TO FIGHT** to be a good wife but didn't ask God for a good husband and didn't set an expectation about what I should receive. I did not measure my husband by God's expectations. God made Christ the head of the church and the husband the head of his wife, but God loves his people. If the husband does not love his wife he doesn't desire that honor talked about. He can't be my head, if he does not love me as God loves the church. Those facts released me from my bondage.

Does submission mean that her husband has complete authority in every decision-making process? Does it mean he makes all the financial decisions and controls all the money? Does it mean she accepts his name-calling and insults? "Stupid b----! F------ idiot! Where is your brain? Can you think?" Does it mean standing still while he throws objects at her or hits her? Does it mean allowing him to force sex on her (legally, this is rape) anytime he wants, even when she is physically exhausted or sick? Does it mean doing all housework and childcare even when sick or working multiple jobs herself? Does it mean not allowing her friends and family to visit or maybe cutting herself off completely from friends and family? No one tells her what submission "is not" and what headship is.

A careful review of Ephesians 5 and 1 Peter will show that submission does not mean accepting physical violence, verbal abuse, or sexual abuse. According to Catherine Clark and Nancy Nason-Clark in *No Place for Abuse*, "Submission involved carrying out a legitimate obligation of marriage while upholding the freedom to serve Christ.

The aim of submission was not subordination, but conversion; not enabling what is wrong, but persisting in what is right."[4]

They add that "1 Peter is not a blanket call for women to endure abuse. Abusive conduct is never redemptive. Rather, it brings an enablement of sins that are damaging to the souls of both the abuser and victim."[5] Where there is a legal redress for abuse, patient endurance is akin to codependence rather than "heroic" conduct.[5] Allowing her husband to violate laws against assault, rape, child abuse, etc., makes her an accomplice to these crimes and therefore in violation of the scripture that states, "Submit yourselves for the Lord's sake to every human authority: whether the emperor, as the supreme authority, or to governors, who are sent by him to punish those who do wrong and to commend those who do right" (1 Peter 2:13–14, NIV).

In addition, the discussion in 1 Peter about submission to any authority (including the husband) did not mean absolute obedience. Obedience to God always has highest priority. Christians' obedience was never meant to violate God's laws or the individual's conscience.[6]

The husband is not the lord of the abused woman's life; Jesus is. Obedience to God's law takes precedence over submitting to her husband's abusive actions. Ephesians 5:21 clarifies the intent of Ephesians 5:22–24 by stating, "Submit to one another out of reverence for Christ." In addition, all Christians— not just wives—are called to submit. If the husband is a Christian, he also is called to a form of submission toward his wife.

> Husbands, love your wives, just as Christ loved the church and gave himself up for her to make her holy, cleansing her by the washing with water through the word, to present her to himself as a radiant church, without stain or wrinkle or any other blemish, but holy and blameless. In this same way, husbands ought to love their wives as their own bodies. He who loves his wife loves himself. After all, no one ever hated his own body, but he feeds and cares for it, just as Christ does the church for we are members of his body. For this reason a man will leave his father and mother and be united to his wife, and the two will become one flesh. This is a profound mystery—but

Spiritual Dilemmas

I am talking about Christ and the church. However, each one of you also must love his wife as he loves himself, and the wife must respect her husband. (Ephesians 5:25–33, NIV)

The last sentence of this scripture makes it clear that the husband and wife relationship is reciprocal. The husband is called to sacrifice as much as or more than the wife. The husband is given the authority by God to lead the family, but this means loving, protecting, and serving the family, not destroying it (Ephesians 5:25–33; Matthew 20:25–28). He is called to spiritually nourish the family so that they can follow Christ.

Biblical Justification for Separation and Divorce

She searches the scriptures to justify her desire to leave the marriage and escape the abuse, but finds none. In 1 Corinthians 7:10–11 conflict is created by stating, "To the married I give this command (not I, but the Lord): A wife must not separate from her husband. But if she does, she must remain unmarried or else be reconciled to her husband." If she separates, the goal is reconciliation. To complicate her dilemma, if she decides to divorce, she must not remarry.

The scriptures also say that if her husband decides to leave she is not bound to the relationship:

> But if the unbeliever leaves, let him do so. A believing man or woman is not bound in such circumstances; God has called us to live in peace. How do you know, wife, whether you will save your husband? Or, how do you know husband, whether you will save your wife? (1 Corinthians 7:15–16, NIV)

She prays that he will leave but he never does, so she stays, hoping that God will change him.

Not only does she feel responsible for the salvation of her non-believer husband, but also for the salvation of her children. This thought is reinforced in the same chapter:

> And if a woman has a husband who is not a believer and he is willing to live with her, she must not divorce him. For

the unbelieving husband has been sanctified through his wife, and the unbelieving wife has been sanctified through her believing husband. Otherwise your children would be unclean, but as it is they are holy. (1 Corinthians 7:13–14, NIV)

Her interpretation of scriptures creates fear, especially when she contemplates divorce. Malachi 2:16 states that God hates divorce. Divorce is confirmed in 1 Corinthians 7 as is a violation of God's law. If she chooses to leave, she will be disobeying the scriptures, and she fears that her decision might destroy her relationship with God. She also fears being put out of the church if she insists on divorce, especially if she has been advised during couple's counseling to work on reconciliation. Wanting divorce means she is too impatient to wait for God to change her husband.

She searches for permission to leave her marriage from the leadership of the church, but no one will advise her to leave, even though some members of her church have witnessed her husband's abusive behaviors. Her spiritual conflicts and the lack of support hinder her from leaving her abusive relationship.

NANCY

ONE NIGHT MY HUSBAND got so angry that he broke glasses everywhere and I couldn't get all the glass up, the baby was crawling and I and the baby got cut from the pieces that were still being found. I remember deciding that I had enough and that I wanted a divorce and the head of the ministry we were a part of came over. The male leader stood in our baby's room and got in my personal space to tell me that he *never* wanted me to say the word Divorce again. Our church had a 0 divorce rate. I spent the next several years trying desperately to pick up the pieces and love my husband. "Love" covered a multitude of sins.

Spiritual Dilemmas

It is difficult for the Christian woman to consider the option of divorce. Until she develops her own conviction that domestic violence is wrong and is not God's will for her life, it will be difficult for her to leave her abuser. She is not responsible for her husband's salvation and does not help him by covering up his sins. God has given him the freedom of choice and is the one who will work on his salvation. This salvation is not within her power—she is not God. If she decides to leave, she has to trust that God will help her bear the consequences of her choice. Ultimately, it is her choice to leave or stay.

The marital instructions in Corinthians 7 were intended as a guide to normal relationships, not dysfunctional relationships that create conflict with God. Paul was speaking about healthy relationships where the marital vows are intact. He appears to direct his teachings to those who are not in relationships where the wife and the children are in danger.

According to Marie Fortune in *Keeping the Faith*, "Any man who brings violence and abuse is responsible for breaking the marriage covenant that God has blessed. It is the violence that breaks up the marriage and the person who brings it into the relationship is responsible for breaking the relationship. The actual divorce is exposing the truth to others that the marriage has long been destroyed by abuse. When you decide to leave, you are not taking steps to break up the marriage, emotionally that [has] already been done."[7]

The abused woman is taking steps to remove herself and children from a destructive environment to an environment of safety from abuse.[7] The physical and emotional safety of herself and her children is more important than the relationship.

In *No Place for Abuse*, Clark Kroeger and Nason-Clark add, "Often the abuser feels no real need to change because he is convinced that divorce is not an option. He assumes that a good Christian wife is required to remain with him regardless of his treatment of her. Divorce is the least desirable option but sometimes a necessary option. The possibility of divorce reinforces the serious nature of the offense and serves as an incentive for changing behavior."[8]

 **EDITH**

I HAD LEFT MY RELATIONSHIP and was in the process of child custody and child support litigation. I didn't want to think about divorce. I found myself overwhelmed by the process because it was complex and stressful for many reasons. I could not use domestic violence as reason for divorce in the courts because proving it was too difficult. As a Christian, I prayed that my husband would start the divorce process so that I wouldn't have to carry the guilt and spiritual burden of initiating divorce. He never did me the favor. My lawyer knew that, as a Christian woman, I would struggle with the idea of divorce. She was willing to allow me the time I needed to arrive at the decision. The main reason that I delayed my decision was that I wanted my church to validate and support my reason for divorce. I sought advice from church leadership. I remember speaking to a member of my church about my husband's abuse as a reason for leaving. Her response was, "I do agree you shouldn't have to live that way," but "I really can't give you any advice because, as a leader, my role is to help marriages work. I can't advise you on divorce."

After struggling for a year with the decision to file, my lawyer called and told me she was going to submit the paperwork if I didn't make up my mind. It was then that I finally decided to divorce and was willing to bear the consequences. One potential consequence was financial ruin, including the possibility of inheriting my husband's huge financial debt along with the burden of single parenting. But most importantly, I was concerned that I would damage my spiritual walk with God. I had to come to the conviction that God loves me and did not want me to live where abuse was accepted and there was no accountability. I believed that God would reveal whether I had made the wrong decision and I knew he would help me bear the consequences. All I could do was to trust in him and continue to hold to his Word.

DEBBIE

THE SCRIPTURES SAY THAT I can't divorce and if I do I can't remarry. I was heathen if I wanted a divorce. When I asked him to leave, he asked if I was leaving the church. I said I wasn't leaving the church. He said in order to divorce me you have to leave the church, because you can't be a Christian and divorce. I felt he was playing a game. He wanted me to divorce him so I would be labeled a heathen. He wanted to be the victim. I always wanted to prove that I was the victim.

I came to the realization that what kept me in the relationship was not God but the people. It was the fear of letting other women down. As a Christian woman, I was supposed to hold on to the faith. I was supposed to be an example to Christian women and other women in the world. I couldn't let go of my relationship because how can I tell my story of faithfulness if I give up? I had believed that wanting a divorce meant that I was giving up on God and my faith. When I finally achieved clarity, I remember hearing, "God isn't holding you here; people are." Once I figured that out, I was willing to let go. It wasn't God. God is whole. He judges the heart.

My advice to the Christian abused woman is you are worthy. God loves you and he says you are worthy of more. We stay because we think that we are honoring God, but you can't honor God without being whole. Your relationship can't honor God if it is not true. All the scriptures that say the wife is supposed to obey and honor the husband are important, but what about honoring you as a daughter of God? You are his child. I only believed that I was worthy in that way later, after I left my husband. I used to feel like I deserved better, but it wasn't until I left that I believed I was worthy and was able to be free. And it wasn't until my second marriage that I began to understand what those scriptures about marriage really mean and finally appreciate them. It was then that I saw the natural calling of the leadership of the husband. When you see his true love for you, you don't have to tell yourself to follow. It automatically flows. I see the scriptures come alive now and get it, but it started with love.

SUSAN

I REALIZED IF OUR MARRIAGE and my sanity were to survive, a separation would be necessary. After much prayer and after seeking the advice of godly people whom we both respected, I summoned what courage I could and, in the form of a handwritten note (which we still have), asked him to leave. I feared he might not survive the emotional blow of what he would surely perceive as the ultimate personal rejection, but I had to risk losing everything if there was to be any hope of redeeming the marriage.

After he left, I felt immediate relief. For the very first time in years, I felt safe from the evil spirit that seemed to live deep inside him. Walking through our house was no longer like walking through a minefield, with me paranoid that I might step on the tripwire. I was inexpressibly relieved but, at the same time, missed the sweetness that was his and grieved the loss of "the good times" we had shared.

I began seeing a Christian counselor on my own in order to regain perspective and wellness of mind and of spirit. My husband threw himself into Christian counseling as well. He sought the assistance of strong Christian brothers to help him on his journey to wholeness and wellness. He did the hard work of confronting his inner demons, seeking to understand his past, and gaining the tools to become an overcomer, trusting that God would keep his promises.

After seven long months of tears, prayers, and hard work—taking one step forward and sometimes three backward—we reconciled. That was twelve years ago. The journey has not been an easy one, but it was one begun in faith that God, who made all things, could make all things new in our marriage.

We now work through issues, usually in less than an hour that would have taken days if not weeks to get beyond in the past. Our commitment is to help each other make it to heaven. My husband sees his primary role as protector, provider, and guide (what Jesus is for the church—his bride). I see my primary role as his helpmeet, to be his "sustainer" beside him, allowing

> God's love and encouragement to flow through me into him to sustain him as he in turn loves, guides, and protects our marriage and me. We see respect and love as mutual responsibilities of each for the other. Love as described in I Corinthians 13 is the goal in the way we strive to treat each other daily. Leading by loving as God defines it is both his and my responsibility. To truly love each other is to love God.

Susan describes in her story some of the elements of a godly marriage. Helping one other make it to heaven is the primary goal. The roles are clearly defined as in scriptures such as Ephesians 5. Both husband and wife are called to submit to one another out of the reverence for Christ. Mutual love and respect for one other is the bond that sustains the relationship.

When the woman gains clarity from the scriptures that causes her spiritual dilemmas, she will develop a conviction to be comfortable with the decision she makes to stay or leave her abusive relationship.

CHAPTER 4

WHAT DOES THE SCRIPTURE SAY?

In this chapter we will examine the scriptures that relate to domestic violence. We will review scriptures about how abuse is sin and how God views relationships in the context of violence. These scriptures can be studied at any time, whether one is going through the various stages of understanding and healing from domestic violence, or is a member of a community trying to help the abused Christian woman.

Domestic Violence as Sin

Abuse is sin. The Christian woman has to view it as such to be healed. This section focuses on sinful behaviors of the abuser. Let's consider these behaviors and how God responds to them.

Physical Violence

The acts of the flesh are obvious: sexual immorality, impurity and debauchery; idolatry and witchcraft; hatred, discord, jealousy, fits of rage, selfish ambition, dissensions, factions and envy; drunkenness, orgies, and the like. I warn you, as I did before, that those who live like this will not inherit the kingdom of God. (Galatians 5:19–21, NIV)

One of the sinful acts listed in this passage of Galatians is "fits of rage." *The Message* translation is "violent temper." When a man with a violent temper gets angry, his anger takes control of him. He loses his ability to think rationally, which demonstrates that he is dangerous and has the ability to seriously harm or kill without a thought about the consequences. This irrationality creates fear among those who see his temper, particularly his wife, which results in her constantly "walking on egg shells." She tries to diffuse his anger to keep the violence from escalating by doing what he likes, for example, serving only food he likes, keeping a perfect house, or training the kids to be quiet when he is at home.

It is important to note that verbal abuse, which can be as bad as physical violence, can occur when someone is calm and there is no visible expression of rage. He may angrily scream abusive language at his wife and, as he is screaming, he receives a telephone call and instantly changes to a calmer demeanor as he talks on the phone. Anger becomes a tool for abuse, not the cause of the abuse. His fits of rage may be premeditated. It is difficult for the woman to accept that her husband's abusive actions are premeditated. She is searching for logical reasons for his behaviors. She needs to believe that they happen due to reasons such as work-related stress, alcohol, or mental problems. God hates violence and will bring his judgment upon those who are violent:

> I hate a man's covering himself with violence as well as with his garment. (Malachi 2:16, NIV)

> The Lord examines both the righteous and the wicked. He hates those who love violence. He will rain down blazing coals and burning sulfur on the wicked, punishing them with scorching winds. (Psalm 11:5–7, NLT)

> Your fasting ends in quarreling and strife, and in striking each other with wicked fists. You cannot fast as you do today and expect your voice to be heard on high. (Isaiah 58:4, NIV)

The abuser can fast and pray all he wants. If he continues to fight and quarrel, God will not hear his prayers.

Dissensions and Factions

The dissensions and factions described in Galatians 5:19–21 also are characteristic of an abuser. The abuser causes dissensions (conflicts) within the family and factions (divisions) in the wife's relationship with her friends, extended family, and church. For example, he undermines her relationship with her mother, closest friends, or, refuses to allow her time alone to visit her family.

This excerpt from Proverbs describes the abuser:

A scoundrel and villain, who goes about with a corrupt mouth, who winks with his eye, signals with his feet and motions with his fingers, who plots evil with deceit in his heart—*he always stirs up dissension. Therefore disaster will overtake him in an instant; he will suddenly be destroyed without remedy.* (Proverbs 6:12–15, NIV, emphasis mine)

Most abusive men try to create divisions that separate the wife from friends, family, and other sources of support to socially isolate her. Social isolation makes her totally dependent on him for emotional and physical support. She has to wait for him to get home to have some companionship because he is all that she has left.

Pride

All humans struggle with pride, but pride controls the abuser. Psalm 73:6 states, "Therefore, pride is their necklace. They clothe themselves with violence," and God's response to such people is seen in Psalm 5:5, "The arrogant cannot stand in your presence; you hate all who do wrong." The abuser has a need to be right and feel superior in the decision-making process at home and refuses to listen to advice from others. Proverbs 21:24 calls such people mockers: "The proud and arrogant man—'Mocker' is his name; he behaves with overweening pride." Proverbs 26:12 (NIV) adds, "Do you see a man wise in his own eyes? There is more hope for a fool than for him." The abuser's pride rears its head when the wife attempts to participate in the decision-making or parenting or, worse, suggests that they seek help for their relationship. He may turn these conversations into arguments, or he may ignore her and find an underhanded way to get what he wants, regardless of her stated needs or plans. He usually refuses to seek help for the marriage. When she attempts to seek outside help, he tells her, "You can't think for yourself," or "Why do you always let people tell you what to do?" His pride stops the family from seeking the help it desperately needs to survive.

And there is a consequence for those who let pride control their lives: "The Lord detests all the proud of heart. Be sure of this: They will not go unpunished" (Proverbs 15:5, NIV). His pride and refusal to listen to his wife or seek outside help destroy both the family and the abuser.

Verbal Abuse and Coarse Joking

God hates abusive speech:

> You're familiar with the command to the ancients, "Do not murder." I'm telling you that anyone who is so much as angry with a brother or sister is guilty of murder. Carelessly call a brother "idiot!" and you just might find yourself hauled into court. Thoughtlessly yell "stupid!" at a sister and you are on the brink of hellfire. The simple moral fact is that words kill. (Matthew 5:21–22, *The Message*)

The communication process in a home where there is domestic violence is filled with verbal abuse, perverse speech, word-twisting, and coarse joking to achieve control. The abuser makes belittling comments to make his wife feel unintelligent, less human, and not capable of understanding what his intentions are. He might say, "Are you stupid or what?" in response to her ideas or questions. Psalm 10:7–8 states, "They carry a mouthful of hexes, their tongues spit venom like adders. They hide behind ordinary people, then pounce on their victims" (*The Message*). The abuser also twists words so that his wife leaves a conversation questioning her own motives. Psalm 56:5 (NLT) reads, "They are always twisting what I say; they spend their days to harm me." He distorts her words to use them against her. He keeps a record of or even invents past conversations and mistakes on her part as examples of her stupidity, immorality, laziness, such as forgetting to pay a bill, or not washing the dishes when company is coming, etc.

The abuser may joke about his wife's appearance, speech, or ideas in a hurtful way. He also may make threatening comments or engage in aggressive behaviors and then claim that he was playing or joking. Or he may make sexually degrading comments about her, her friends, or women in general. When she becomes upset about these behaviors, his response is, "Can't you take a joke?" Fortunately, God's Word brings reality to the forefront in Proverbs 26:18-19 (NIV): "Like a madman shooting firebrands or deadly arrows is a man who deceives his neighbor and says, 'I was only joking!'" His jokes, however, are intended to belittle or threaten her. These techniques cause her to doubt her thought processes and sanity, causing her to feel worthless.

James 1:26 (NLT) advises Christians, "If you claim to be religious but don't control your tongue, you are fooling yourself, and your religion is worthless." Christians also are instructed in Ephesians 4:29 (NIV), "Do not let any unwholesome talk come out of your mouths, but only what is helpful for building others up according to their needs, that it may benefit those who listen," and the next chapter continues: "Nor should there be obscenity, foolish talk or coarse joking, which are out of place . . ." (Ephesians 5:4, NIV). If the husband claims to be a Christian, he cannot routinely engage in verbal abuse and coarse language, particularly with his wife.

Lies and Deceptions

Lies and deception are an integral part of the abuser's behavior. He only can continue his abusive behavior by deceiving those around him. Over time, however, most abused women become complicit in the deception that surrounds the abuse. This section, therefore, focuses on the sin of deception on the part of both the abusive husband and the abused wife.

"Do not lie. Do not deceive one another" we read in Leviticus 19:11 (NIV). The abusive relationship is filled with lies and deceptions. Things are not what they seem. Both partners are wearing masks. The painting "Face Reality" by Laurie Cooper illustrates to me the masks worn in an abusive relationship. This painting of a male and female wearing masks shows the male looking directly at the viewer, his eyes open, and an intense expression on his face. With control, he meticulously peels off his mask a tiny piece at a time with one hand. The woman, on the other hand, has her eyes closed and her mask is falling off even as she tries desperately to hold it to her face. Inevitably, her mask will come tumbling off.

The Abuser's Deception

The abuser wears his mask and is in control as he exposes what he wants others to see. He wants everyone to see how great he is—how he is a great husband and father. He keeps a record of all the great things he does for the family. He may boast about the gifts he gives his family. He may seem like a fun, easygoing guy or a hardworking, responsible family man. At home he is different—cool, distant, easily irritated, and emotionally and physically abusive:

> A malicious man disguises himself with his lips, but in his heart he harbors *deceit*. Though his speech is charming, do not believe him, for seven abominations fill his heart. His malice may be concealed by *deception*, but his wickedness will be exposed in the assembly. (Proverbs 26:24–26, NIV, emphasis mine)

And Psalm 55:21 (NIV) adds, "His speech is smooth as butter, yet war is in his heart; his words are more soothing than oil, yet they are drawn swords."

The abuser also is deceptive about his motive. He will give all kinds of reasons for his abusive behavior, but will never admit his true motive—control. Lundy Bancroft, author of *Why Does He Do That? Inside the Minds of Angry and Controlling Men*, states:

> The abusive man works like a magician. He tricks you to look in the wrong direction, distracting you so you cannot see where the real action is. He wants you to focus on his chaotic world of feelings to keep your eyes turned away from the real cause of his abuse, which lies in how he *thinks*. He leads you in a complicated maze with many twists and turns. He wants you to puzzle over him, to figure him out. His desire is that

you wrack your brain and not notice the pattern and logic of his behavior, the consciousness behind his craziness. If you could follow the thread of his conduct in past relationships, you will begin to see that his behavior is not erratic as it looks; it follows a consistent pattern. Above all, the abusive man does not want you to see his abusive tendencies, so he tries to fill your head with excuses and distractions to keep you weighed down in self-doubt and self-blame.[1]

God hates deceptions and lies, as noted in scriptural passages such as these:

> You destroy those who tell lies; bloodthirsty and deceitful men the Lord abhors. (Psalm 5:6, NIV)

> Here are six things God hates, and one more that he loathes with a passion: eyes that are arrogant, *a tongue that lies*, hands that murder the innocent, a heart that hatches evil plots, feet that race down a wicked track, a mouth that lies under oath, a troublemaker in the family. (Proverbs 6:16, *The Message*, emphasis mine).

The Abused Woman's Deception

The woman's mask is falling off, yet she still tries to control what she wants others to see. She pretends that everything is normal and attempts to control what is happening at home so others will not see her humiliation. She is afraid to speak the truth about what is going on at home because of her fear that he will hurt her or because of her guilt, shame, and a sense of failure. As she loses control, her pain, shame, and humiliation are visible for all to see. She may keep the abuse secret until signs of the violence are visible. At this point, she can no longer hide the abuse and her mask begins to crumble. The reality is that she attempts to control what she has no control of.

The Christian woman must consider how the abuse creates her own mask of deception, which damages her spiritual life. An abused woman usually feels compelled to *cover up* or minimize the abuse.

Although she may not be aware that she is doing this, it is deceitful. This deceit is sin, and *any* sin creates a separation from God. Once the woman removes her mask and exposes the abuse, she can begin to heal and reconcile with God.

To do this, she must speak the whole truth. "Jesus said, 'If you hold to my teaching, you are really my disciples. Then you will know the truth, and the truth will set you free'" (John 8:31–32, NIV). Jesus promises the Christian woman that if she holds on to his teachings, she will know the truth and the truth will set her free. In other words, she has to reveal the abuse for what it is, speak the truth, and the truth will set her free.

So Who Is Responsible?

The scriptures are clear about abuse. They place the responsibility of the abuse on the abuser. The victim does not have the power to stop the abuse, the abuser does. She does, however, have the power to expose the abuse and the moral responsibility to do so. If the sins of abuse are not dealt with, they destroy both the victim and the abuser physically and spiritually. Dealing with sin involves repentance. The husband is responsible for producing "fruit in keeping with repentance" (Matthew 3:8). The wife is responsible for bringing her abuse into the light: "Arise, shine, for your light has come, and the glory of the Lord rises upon you. See, darkness covers the earth and thick darkness is over the peoples, but the Lord rises upon you and his glory appears over you" (Isaiah 60:1–2, NIV).

She should not be ashamed to speak the truth, for the Lord has chosen her to show His glory. The Christian woman can no longer hide or allow the abuse to dim her light:

> You are the light of the world. A town built on a hill cannot be hidden. Neither do people light a lamp and put it under a bowl. Instead, they put it on its stand and it gives light to everyone in the house. In the same way, let your light shine before others, that they may see your good deeds and glorify your Father in heaven. (Matthew 5:14–16, NIV)

Examining the Scriptures about Relationships

The Bible provides many stories about different people's lives in order to teach Christians which behaviors to imitate or which to avoid. Often these stories are taken out of context, leading to internal conflicts, particularly for the Christian woman who is in an abusive relationship. She has difficulty applying stories about marriages in the scriptures to her own relationship. These stories provoke feelings of inadequacy. Internal conflicts are created when she is told, "Wasn't Abigail's husband a mean man, yet she didn't leave but tried to save her husband's life?" or Sarah called her husband "My Master." 1 Peter 3:6 teaches that we are daughters of Sarah, and we as women are to follow in her footsteps. Married Christian women generally are taught to imitate Abigail and Sarah.

In this section, we will look at the stories of Abigail and Sarah to help the abused woman develop her own convictions. We will use examples from these biblical women's stories to change her perceptions about her abuse.

The Stories

ABIGAIL

A certain man in Maon, who had property there at Carmel, was very wealthy. He had a thousand goats and three thousand sheep, which he was shearing in Carmel. His name was Nabal and his wife's name was Abigail. She was an intelligent and beautiful woman, but her husband was surly and mean in his dealings—he was a Calebite.

While David was in the wilderness, he heard that Nabal was shearing sheep. So he sent ten young men and said to them, "Go up to Nabal at Carmel and greet him in my name. Say to him: 'Long life to you! Good health to you and your household! And good health to all that is yours! 'Now I hear that it is sheep-shearing time. When your shepherds were with us, we did not mistreat them, and the whole time they were at Carmel nothing of theirs was missing. Ask your own servants and they will tell you. Therefore be favorable toward my men, since we come at a festive time. Please give your servants and your son David whatever you can find for them.'"

When David's men arrived, they gave Nabal this message in David's name. Then they waited. Nabal answered David's servants, "Who is this David? Who is this son of Jesse? Many servants are breaking away from their masters these days. Why should I take my bread and water, and the meat I have slaughtered for my shearers, and give it to men coming from who knows where?"

David's men turned around and went back. When they arrived, they reported every word. David said to his men, "Each of you strap on your sword!" So they did, and David strapped his on as well. About four hundred men went up with David, while two hundred stayed with the supplies.

One of the servants told Abigail, Nabal's wife, "David sent messengers from the wilderness to give our master his greetings, but he hurled insults at them. Yet these men were very good to us. They did not mistreat us, and the whole time we were out in the fields near them nothing was missing. Night and day they were a wall around us the whole time we were herding our sheep near them. Now think it over and see what you can do, because disaster is hanging over our master and his whole household. He is such a wicked man that no one can talk to him."

Abigail acted quickly. She took two hundred loaves of bread, two skins of wine, five dressed sheep, five seahs of roasted grain, a hundred cakes of raisins and two hundred cakes of pressed figs, and loaded them on donkeys. Then she told her servants, "Go on ahead; I'll follow you." But she did not tell her husband Nabal.

As she came riding her donkey into a mountain ravine, there were David and his men descending toward her, and she met them. David had just said, "It's been useless—all my watching over this fellow's property in the wilderness so that nothing of his was missing. He has paid me back evil for good. May God deal with David, be it ever so severely, if by morning I leave alive one male of all who belong to him!"

When Abigail saw David, she quickly got off her donkey and bowed down before David with her face to the ground. She fell at his feet and said: "Pardon your servant, my lord, and let me speak to you; hear what your servant has to say. Please pay no attention, my lord, to that wicked man Nabal. He is just like his name—his name means Fool, and folly goes with him. And as for me, your servant, I did not see the men my lord sent. And let this gift, which your servant has brought to my lord, be given to the men who follow you.

"Please forgive your servant's presumption. The Lord your God will certainly make a lasting dynasty for my lord, because you fight the Lord's battles, and no wrongdoing will be found in you as long as you live. Even though someone is pursuing you to take your life, the life of my lord will be bound securely in the bundle of the living by the Lord your God, but the lives of your enemies he will hurl away as from the pocket of a sling. When the Lord has fulfilled for my lord every good thing he promised concerning him and has appointed him ruler over Israel, my lord will not have on his conscience the staggering burden of needless bloodshed or of having avenged himself. And when the Lord your God has brought my lord success, remember your servant."

David said to Abigail, "Praise be to the Lord, the God of Israel, who has sent you today to meet me. May you be blessed for your good judgment and for keeping me from bloodshed this day and from avenging myself with my own hands. Otherwise, as surely as the Lord, the God of Israel, lives, who has kept me from harming you, if you had not come quickly to meet me, not one male belonging to Nabal would have been left alive by daybreak."

Then David accepted from her hand what she had brought him and said, "Go home in peace. I have heard your words and granted your request."

When Abigail went to Nabal, he was in the house holding a banquet like that of a king. He was in high spirits and very drunk. So she told him nothing at all until daybreak. Then in the morning, when Nabal was sober, his wife told him all these things, and his heart failed him and he became like a stone. About ten days later, the Lord struck Nabal and he died.

When David heard that Nabal was dead, he said, "Praise be to the Lord, who has upheld my cause against Nabal for treating me with contempt. He has kept his servant from doing wrong and has brought Nabal's wrongdoing down on his own head." (1 Samuel 25:2–38, NIV)

Considering the Story

Let's examine Nabal's character and compare it with abuser characteristics. In the NLT, Nabal is described as "crude and mean" in all his dealings. Nabal is verbally abusive—"he screamed insults at them." Ill-tempered and out of control emotionally, he refuses to listen to anyone and makes it difficult for others to approach him.

"He is such a wicked man that no one can even talk to him." Pride controls his actions. "Who is this David? Who is this son of Jesse? Many servants are breaking away from their masters these days. Why should I take my bread and water, and the meat I have slaughtered for my shearers, and give it to men coming from who knows where?" And apparently he has an inflated ego: "He was in the house holding a banquet like that of a king."

Do you see these abusive characteristics in Nabal's personality? Is Nabal abusive to Abigail? The scriptures do not state that he abuses Abigail, but based on his character, one can infer that he may have. There is a high probability that, if a person is verbally abusive outside the home, he also will be abusive within the home.

Abigail is beautiful and intelligent. The servants trust her ability to make good decisions. They know that, compared to her husband, she is rational in her thinking. "Now think it over and see what you can do, because disaster is hanging over our master and his whole household." She is a great problem-solver and she considers what is best for her whole household.

Abigail has the power to mobilize household resources quickly to provide food for David and his men. She has and uses the authority to take household resources without Nabal's consent; just think of what she is quickly able to bring to David as a peace offering. She must have had these in storage: bread, wine, sheep, grains, raisins, and figs.

For Abigail, protecting the household takes precedence over obedience to Nabal's irrational wishes. By acting without Nabal's consent and approaching David when he is on verge of attacking her household, she accepts great personal risk on two fronts: first, Nabal likely would have reacted violently when he found out what she did; second, David himself acknowledges that he could have killed Abigail as she approached him.

Abigail isn't afraid to acknowledge the truth about her husband's character, even to a stranger, admitting to David that Nabal is wicked and ill-tempered. She even calls him a fool.

Nabal's behaviors indicate he is not following the Jewish tradition of hospitality, which calls for one to be hospitable to travelers, especially those who have assisted with harvesting.

However, Abigail does not let her husband's lack of faith affect her beliefs. Her faith is her own, and it influences her to do the right thing.

Abigail is strongly convinced that David is a man of God and that God has promised to protect David and take revenge on his enemies. She persuades David to do the right thing by not attacking the innocent and by allowing God to take vengeance, predicting that God will make of his lineage "a lasting dynasty," that "no wrongdoing will be found in you as long as you live," and that God will "hurl away" all his enemies.

Abigail is not afraid to tell Nabal what had happened, but uses wisdom by waiting until he is sober. God protects Abigail and does not let Nabal's actions go unnoticed. Ten days later, "the Lord struck him dead." Nabal has to pay the consequences of his actions. In this case, that consequence is death.

What can the abused Christian woman learn from Abigail's story?
- To make the protection of her household a priority over obedience to an irrational and violent husband. The abused Christian woman is responsible for protecting her family from abuse. She has the moral and legal right and the responsibility to seek help from available and legitimate sources, including law enforcement or the courts.

- Abigail did not need permission to do the right thing. The abused Christian woman often is told she is her husband's helper and needs permission from him for any decision. But she does not need permission from the abuser to protect her children or herself.
- Abigail was not afraid to call her husband's character what it was—wicked and ill-tempered, a fool. The abused Christian woman should not be afraid to call her relationship what it is—"abusive"—and to call her husband an "abuser." Giving a name to the problem will communicate to others that the problem is real and empower her to expose the abuse and seek help.
- Abigail's faith was her own. She was aware of the promises God had made to David to rule Israel and went to David, trusting that God would protect her. The abused Christian woman should examine the scriptures for herself and not be influenced by others' interpretations. She must develop her own convictions before she can move toward change. The Word of God alone can give her the spiritual strength she needs to break the bondage of domestic violence.
- God punished Nabal for his actions. The abused Christian woman should find comfort in the fact that God is on her side and that her abuser will pay the consequences for his actions.

SARAH

Sarah often is held up as an example of the ideal behavior of the Christian wife, particularly during difficult times in the marriage. Scriptures throughout the Bible, in both the New and Old Testaments, refer to Sarah and her example of wifely submission. Because these scriptures appear in different parts of the Bible, this discussion of Sarah is organized by key points.

Sarah and Abraham's relationship was defined by mutual respect. Sarah calls her husband, Abraham, her master, out of respect for him: "...like Sarah, who obeyed Abraham and called him her master" (1 Peter 3:6, NIV). Despite the term "master," her relationship is not the same as that of a slave to a master. Instructing the Christian woman to follow the example of Sarah doesn't mean that she should allow her husband to treat her like a slave. As we examine Sarah's story, there is no evidence of abuse. There is no indication that Abraham mistreats Sarah. Sarah's relationship with Abraham is based on their mutual respect and support for one another. Abraham loves his wife and listens to her input in the decision-making process, as is evident in his interactions with her.

Sarah's faith was her own. Sarah is placed in an environment that is hostile to her faith. She is taken to a strange place where people worship idols. Abraham acts out of fear and doesn't trust God, so he asks Sarah to lie to protect him. Sarah is obedient and follows her husband's instructions. She is left alone to face the situation, with no protection from her husband:

> Now there was a famine in the land, and Abram went down to Egypt to live there for a while because the famine was severe. As he was about to enter Egypt, he said to his wife Sarai, "I know what a beautiful woman you are. When the Egyptians see you, they will say, 'This is his wife.' Then they will kill me but will let you live. Say you are my sister, so that I will be treated well for your sake and my life will be spared because of you." (Genesis 12:10–13, NIV)

Sarah has to depend on God for her protection. She has to trust that God will deliver her, and he does. As a result of Sarah's faithfulness,

> The Lord inflicted serious diseases on Pharaoh and his household because of Abram's wife Sarai. So Pharaoh summoned Abram. "What have you done to me?" he said. "Why didn't you tell me she was your wife? Why did you say, 'She is my sister,' so that I took her to be my wife? Now then, here is your wife. Take her and go!" Then Pharaoh gave orders about Abram to his men, and they sent him on his way, with his wife and everything he had. (Genesis 12:17–20, NIV)

Like Sarah's, the abused woman's faith is her own. She may find herself all alone with no one to protect her or no resources, but God is there. He will always be by her side and will never leave her.

Abraham listened to Sarah. Abraham does not pursue a second wife on his own. There also is no indication that he demands heirs. Sarah, however, desires children. Abraham sleeps with Hagar to conceive an heir because of his wife's request:

> Now Sarai, Abram's wife, had borne him no children. But she had an Egyptian slave named Hagar; so she said to Abram, "The Lord has kept me from having children. Go, sleep with my slave; perhaps I can build a family through her." Abram agreed to what Sarai said. So after Abram had been living in Canaan ten years, Sarai his wife took her Egyptian slave Hagar and gave her to her husband to be his wife. He slept with Hagar, and she conceived. (Genesis 16:1-4, NIV)

Sarah ultimately has a child of her own and the Bible says:

> The child grew and was weaned, and on the day Isaac was weaned Abraham held a great feast. But Sarah saw that the son whom Hagar the Egyptian had borne to Abraham was mocking, and she said to Abraham, "Get rid of that slave woman and her son, for that woman's son will never share in the inheritance with my son Isaac." The matter distressed Abraham greatly because it concerned his son. But God said to him, "Do not be so distressed about the boy and your slave woman. Listen to whatever Sarah tells you, because it is through Isaac that your offspring will be reckoned. I will make the son of the slave into a nation also, because he is your offspring." (Genesis 21: 1-13, NIV)

Abraham doesn't agree with Sarah's request, but has to be obedient because God instructed him to follow her request and assured him that both Isaac and his other son would produce nations.

What can the abused Christian woman learn from Sarah?
Catherine Clark Kroegar and Nancy Nason-Clark in *No Place for Abuse,* highlight several lessons from the life of Sarah:

- The community must help women to understand that they have the God-given right to make moral and spiritual decisions.
- Women must answer to God and not to their husband, relatives, or faith communities.
- Like Sarah, women are called to strike out in a new direction.
- Like Sarah, women may find it necessary to insist that their children do not live in abusive or potentially abusive situations.
- Like Sarah, women must act on their concern for their children's and their own safety.
- As with Sarah, God may ultimately support a woman's decision, even if it conflicts with her husband's wishes.[2]

As the abused Christian woman examines stories of the lives of Sarah and Abigail, she will gain wisdom and insight into the many ways that Abigail and Sarah were women worthy of imitating. Both of these women were strong, relied on God, and knew how to make demands to ensure the welfare of their households and themselves.

PART THREE

Lessons for Healing

CHAPTER 5

CHOOSING TO HEAL AND HOPE AGAIN

Whether an abused Christian woman decides to leave her relationship or stay, she must make the choice to heal and regain her hope in God. To start the healing process, she has to go through a process of self-evaluation. She then must make the choice to heal. As part of this process, she learns to take personal responsibility for changing what she can and letting go of what is not her responsibility. Finally, she relearns hope and trust in God's promises.

Self-Evaluation

Self-evaluation involves examining how she got into and chose to stay in her abusive relationship as well as its effects on physical and emotional wellbeing. Accepting the facts of her abuse and its effects, forgiving herself and others, and making the decision to seek change is needed to complete her healing process.

Why did I get into this mess?

By knowing the choices that led her to become the victim of an abuser, the woman is empowered to make better choices in the future. Discovering how she got into an abusive relationship and why she continued to accept the abuse also is necessary to start the healing process.

The woman may have entered and remained in the relationship because she loved her husband. She will have to reevaluate her perception of love and consider how the abuse led her to develop a faulty concept of what love is. As she moves on her path of healing, this faulty concept of love must change and be replaced with a healthy and biblical view of love.

She must acknowledge that she made many decisions based on fear. She may have feared for herself or her family's safety or security, or she may have feared a sense of failure and/or rejection by family members, friends, the church, or even God. Any or all of these reasons may have played a role in her decision to remain in the relationship.

It may be difficult to accept that she allowed her fears to stop her from seeking help and taking responsibility for her situation. And once she accepts these choices, she must go through the difficult process of learning to overcome those fears and move forward. To overcome her fears, she must first determine if they are rational or irrational and then conquer them with truths and facts.

Shame may be second only to fear as a primary reason why women do not expose abuse and work toward changing their situation. Shame is especially destructive because it damages one's sense of self. Shame can be self-inflicted, as opposed to embarrassment, which is more related to a concern about others' perceptions. Shame especially affects educated women who "ought to know better," women who have resources that normally would protect them, and women who are used to being in control.

The abused woman feels ashamed about her helplessness and the fact that she allowed her husband to insult and belittle her. Her shame is increased by the embarrassment that she experiences. She may take extreme measures to avoid embarrassment by covering up her abuse and pretending that everything is okay at home. When she leaves the relationship, that embarrassment may stop her from revealing the details of the abuse, which hampers her healing. The shame, on the other hand, damages her self-worth, which may further impede her healing. Exposing and communicating her shame in a safe environment and in the presence of God will help her to start her healing process.

As the woman considers the reasons she got into and remained in an abusive relationship, painful emotions will resurface. Friends might have told her that she allowed him to abuse her. That statement, although misguided, has some element of truth. In the beginning of the relationship, she allowed him to cross certain boundaries and did not stop him. As he kept pushing, her boundaries diminished further.

>  **DEBBIE**
>
> **I WANTED TO AVOID** the label or stigma that goes with being in an abusive relationship. I also had to fight my family because of my beliefs. To accept that I was wrong was hard. I had to release the voices of others and listen to the voice in me. Shutting out the other voices was hard. I had to search to decide who I wanted to be. I had to ask myself "What is my purpose and mission to this world?" "Who do I want to be?" I knew who I was then. I knew I did not want to be the opposite of who I was. I had to seek healing before entering another relationship.
>
> How does the abuse continue to affect me?

A woman who has left the marriage, as she self-reflects, might ask herself questions like, "Why didn't I leave early?" "I can't believe I let him treat me that way. Why didn't I do something sooner?" These types of questions produce anger and regret. Anger itself is not all bad. For example, her anger might lead her to determine "I will never let anyone treat me this way again." She has the right to be angry about the injustices that she endured. Being angry may have empowered her to seek change. But if anger over time is not dealt with, it can affect her interactions with others, with herself, and, most importantly, with God.

As she moves forward, the woman may realize that her abuse has hampered her ability to trust others. She must learn to use wisdom in dealing with unsafe people like her abuser, while learning to trust other people as well. She may find that she has difficulty trusting God because he appears to have allowed her abuse. As she works on healing, she must learn to regain her trust in God, which will help restore her trust in others.

It is important to note that a Christian woman is not required to trust her abuser, who may be unsafe. Trust is earned. Her abuser must repent and demonstrate by his behaviors that he is trustworthy. This process will not occur overnight, even if he is receiving counseling. Many abusive men will never be safe.

NANCY

I RECALL DURING MY HEALING, I would write lists of it (the abuse) so that I would not forget, as it is so easy to do. My mind never wanted to remember. I was so quick to forget. Only when I could keep that list in front of me could I say no to such evil.

Amazing power the abuse has, somehow it was so woven with my intense hopes and dreams that I kept believing the lie that everything was OK. I was so desperate for love and to be loved, for a happy ending that I stayed for far longer than made sense. I still have to remind myself and have friends remind me of what kind of person he is to me, to this day I keep thinking he'll be nice to me and it never happens. With kids, losing custody to him means the abuse continues and it sickens me most days. He has been given ultimate power and control, the courts allowed him to win the final battle and he gloats as he took away recent visits just because he can. I'm not sure if or when the nightmare will end. The good news is that the nightmares consume less of my waking time and my dreams at night. I remember the first night I slept through the night peacefully because he was not there or rather, I was not there. I had escaped and I felt like a newborn baby, sleeping so sound and so peacefully. I pray that every woman can have that sleep and that somehow the nightmare that will likely remain part of our society for some time can be lessened by the knowledge that we are not alone. That dear women everywhere, some in our own backyards, need our hands, our hearts and our souls to reach out and offer healing and direction on how to come home to themselves—to finally be safe and sound.

Acceptance, Forgiveness, and Moving Forward

For the abused woman, forgiveness of those who have hurt her is critical to moving forward and healing. Her greatest challenge as she seeks healing is self-forgiveness. It will be easier to forgive others, even her abuser, than it will be to forgive herself. To complete the healing process, however, self-forgiveness is essential. She will need to understand and accept God's love and grace—this is the key to self-forgiveness. She will need a lot of prayers for surrender in this area. She must remember that it takes time to achieve emotional healing.

It is important to remember that the Word of God has the power to change and heal. This means that the woman who wants to heal must read the Word of God, believe it, and obey it. It may be necessary for her to study the Bible with others to strengthen her faith.

The woman must examine her relationship with God. Does she have a close relationship with him? Does she understand his Word well enough to apply it to her life to get healing? Is her faith strong or weak? This step in the healing process will require much prayer on a daily basis, as well as the prayers of other faithful people.

The Power Is in the Choice (Healing Is a Choice)

Lesson 1

In working through this lesson, the abused Christian woman will discover that the power is in the choice! God has given her "free will." When she made the choice to follow Christ, she made her first decision for change and freedom. When she decides to end her bondage to abuse, she makes another important decision for change and growth—receiving her healing. Each of these choices requires much courage, strength, careful thought, and prayer.

But before she can move forward, the woman must examine her attitudes and behaviors that are stumbling blocks to change. Let's examine the story of the lame man in John 5:1–9. In the story hundreds of sick people lay around the pool waiting for a particular movement of the water by an angel. To get healed of diseases or deformities, however, the sick person had to do something, in this case, step into the pool first after it had been stirred by the angel. Like the lame man in the story, the abused Christian woman cannot simply wait for God to change her situation; God expects her to act.

The Story
THE LAME MAN BY THE POOL

Here's the story:

Afterward Jesus returned to Jerusalem for one of the Jewish holy days. Inside the city, near the Sheep Gate, was the pool of Bethesda, with five covered porches. Crowds of sick people—blind, lame, or paralyzed—lay on the porches. One of the men lying there had been sick for thirty-eight years. When Jesus saw him and knew he had been ill for a long time, he asked him, "Would you like to get well?" "I can't, sir," the sick man said, "for I have no one to put me into the pool when the water bubbles up. Someone else always gets there ahead of me." Jesus told him, "Stand up, pick up your mat, and walk!" Instantly, the man was healed! He rolled up his sleeping mat and began walking! (John 5:1–9, NLT)

Considering the story and how it applies to the abused Christian woman:

This man had been sick for thirty-eight years! The scripture does not reveal the nature of the man's illness. Some of his possible afflictions could be multiple trauma or accident, infection, or birth defect. His affliction may have been the result of some choice he made (e.g., getting into a fight, not treating an infection). The abused Christian woman, like this man, may have made some choices that led her to seek change or healing. Domestic violence has affected her life. Like this man, she is looking for an opportunity to change her situation.

What do you think kept this man from receiving his healing for more than thirty-eight years? He believed getting into this huge pool with its five covered porches would heal him, but he never got in. Something was blocking him from getting into the pool. The abused woman also may feel unable to take action to make changes and receive healing from her abuse. In order to move forward, she will have to examine her past and the character traits that hindered her from seeking change.

What might have hindered the lame man from getting in the pool? First, he might have lacked motivation. Certainly, his disability was an important barrier that made it difficult to get into the pool. On the other hand, with a lot of determination he might have dragged himself to the edge of the pool. But this act would require a lot of physical and emotional effort and might even be physically painful.

In order to change, the abused woman must be willing to put forth some effort. This process will require physical and emotional effort and spiritual struggle. The healing process will require further struggle, including revisiting her past and talking about the abuse. Both the process of change and the process of healing are likely to be painful. Talking about the abuse she endured will be especially painful because it will open old wounds and expose her shame. She will have to reflect on what brought her into and kept her in the relationship. This reflection will allow her to understand her role in changing her situation and take responsibility for her own healing.

Another reason that the lame man had not received healing might have been that he did not have a plan for getting into the pool. His conversation with Jesus suggests that for thirty-eight years he had not thought about a way to get into the pool. How long had he considered trying the pool? Could he gradually have worked his way to the edge of the pool? He found a way to eat, shelter himself, and otherwise survive for thirty-eight years, yet he had no plan for moving a few feet!

If the abused woman decides to leave her husband, it is important to for her to develop a plan before leaving. That means developing a safety plan, finding financial resources, and knowing where to go for physical and psychological support. Healing also requires a plan.

The Christian woman who wishes to heal has to have a plan for coping with the psychological effects of the abuse. She has to learn to reject the lies that she has come to believe about herself and her abuse. She must apply scriptures to counter these lies (e.g., that she is responsible for the abuse or deserves it). As mentioned earlier, she must work on building her faith and understanding God's character and how to embrace his promises. That means intense prayer, Bible study, and asking for spiritual guidance.

A third reason that the lame man could not receive healing might be that he blamed others for not getting well. He says: "…for I have no one to put me into the pool when the water bubbles up. Someone else always gets there ahead of me."

The abused woman must take responsibility for seeking change and healing from her abuse. She cannot wait for a "knight in shining armor" to come to her physical or emotional rescue. She cannot expect others to reach out to her; she must reach out to them for help. She also cannot blame others for keeping her in the abusive situation. For example, a woman may receive misguided advice to return to an abuser and continue to accept his abuse. Although the person who provides this type of advice has responsibility for his or her error, the woman chose to take the advice and must accept that this ultimately was her decision.

Fear likely was another factor in the lame man's failure to get into the pool. He may have feared for his physical safety (getting pushed and injured by others at the pool). He also may have feared healing. Healing would require him to completely change the way he had lived for the past thirty-eight years. He would have to learn how to care for and support himself.

The abused woman may fear change and healing for some of the same reasons. The number one reason she may stay in her abusive relationship is fear. Many abused women naturally fear for their own safety and the safety of their children when they leave the abuser because the abuse is likely to escalate at this point.[1] She, too, may fear change and healing because this will force her to change a familiar way of living even if it is painful. She also will need to change familiar but self-destructive beliefs and behaviors. These fears, however, stop the woman from living the life that God intended.

The lame man also did not ask for help. Perhaps he did not have close relationships: "I have no one to help." Nevertheless, he was surrounded by others who could have helped. He did not even ask Jesus for help. Jesus had to approach him.

The abused woman has a tendency not to seek help. Alone, she attempts to resolve problems associated with the abuse. She needs the support and resources of others to change her situation. Her family, friends, the secular community, and the church all have important roles in helping her to change and heal. She has to develop the conviction that it is her right, even her obligation, to seek help, especially when her home is not safe. As noted earlier, she also cannot heal alone.

How did Jesus respond to the lame man? Jesus knew of this man's history and failures, yet he placed the power to choose healing in his hands. Jesus asked him, "Would you like to get well?"

It does not make any difference what the abused woman did in the past. She may have accepted the abuse, covered it up, failed to trust God, or even allowed her children to be abused. Jesus still places the power to change and heal in her hands.

When the woman has done her part, like the lame man, she will need faith to move forward. Jesus said to the man, "Stand up, pick up your sleeping mat, and walk!" The man had to trust Jesus. His desire to walk became so great that he chose to overcome all his fears, take the leap of faith, stand up, pick up his mat, and walk.

The woman also has to reach a point when her need to end her abuse becomes her highest priority. She must be willing to overcome fears and pain, take a leap of faith by trusting Jesus, pick herself up, and move forward!

Self-Reflection

Read John 5:1-9 again and consider the following questions:

1. What is blocking you or hindering you from moving forward to free yourself from the bondage of domestic abuse? Even if you are out of the relationship, what psychological or spiritual bondage do you continue to experience? Write down your thoughts. It is important that you educate yourself about the dynamic of domestic abuse before moving forward in the healing process. (See Chapter 2.)

2. Until this time, what interfered with your seeking help to end your abuse? How many times did you think about exposing the abuse, getting help, or leaving, and then stop? What specific thoughts made you stop, hesitate, or change your mind? For example, you may have thought, "I cannot support my children alone." If you have already left the abusive relationship, how can you take responsibility for your decisions and make better ones in the future? If you still are in an abusive relationship, what areas of your life can you control to improve your situation? Realize that the abuser is not someone you can change. Areas you might be able to change could include obtaining job training, making a safety plan, seeking help and support from others.

3. What excuses did you make or are you making for remaining in an abusive situation? Common excuses might include, "I have

no one to help me," "I have no money," "He needs me," "My kids need a father."

4. What physical and psychological effects of the abuse have you experienced? Have you learned about the possible effects of abuse (e.g., insomnia, low self-esteem, restlessness, depression, anxiety, etc.)? Consider what you can do to heal from these effects. Acknowledge issues that you cannot handle on your own. Bring what you cannot change to God. You may need to seek professional help to overcome effects of abuse that are interfering with your ability to function as a parent, worker, friend, etc. For any symptoms of mental illness such as suicidal ideation, please seek professional help.

5. If you are in an abusive relationship and contemplating leaving, do you have a plan? If you plan to stay in your relationship, do you have a plan to ensure the safety of yourself and your children and to deal with the emotional effects of the abuse? If you left the abuser, do you have a plan for healing? Whatever your decision or situation, you need to research the resources available for abused women in your area to develop an effective plan.

6. Do you have a close relationship with God? If not, do you desire to know him more fully? Your plan may need to include working on your relationship with God as you seek healing.

7. Have you given up trying to change your life? Be honest with yourself (if you are using this book in a group, you do not need to share this with others). What caused you to give up or see your situation as hopeless? Do you believe that you deserve what is happening or that you have no other options? Do you feel overwhelmed or paralyzed by fear? List your fears and doubts. You can overcome these fears and doubts by bringing them to God and others.

8. Is your need for change so great that you are willing to do whatever is needed? Are you willing to put your past behind you and trust Jesus to help you move forward? The *power to change* is in your hands!

Taking Action to Heal: Scriptures for Encouragement

"Anyone who belongs to Christ has become a new person. The old life is gone; the new has begun!" (2 Corinthians 5:17, NLT). Today can be the day that the old goes away and a new way of thinking can come. The old way of looking at your life and situation must change. You were renewed in Christ. Therefore, get rid of the old way you see yourself.

Embrace how God sees you! Your new way of thinking must reflect his thinking. Don't accept and cover up the sins of your abuser. As a new person in Christ be Christ's ambassador for what is righteous.

"Be strong and courageous, and do the work. Don't be afraid or discouraged, for the Lord God, my God is with you. He will not fail you or forsake you" (1 Chronicles 28:20, NLT). Be strong and courageous and seek change and healing. It will be a difficult task, but don't be afraid or discouraged. God is with you and he will never fail you or leave you.

"So I say to you: Ask and it will be given to you; seek and you will find; knock and the door will be opened to you. For everyone who asks receives; the one who seeks finds; and to the one who knocks, the door will be opened" (Luke 11:9–10, NIV). Don't be afraid to ask God for what you need. He is willing to listen and will answer you. Also ask for help from others. God uses people as his instrument to answer your prayers.

"Come to me, all you who are weary and burdened, and I will give you rest. Take my yoke upon you and learn from me, for I am gentle and humble in heart, and you will find rest for your souls. For my yoke is easy and my burden is light" (Matthew 11:28–30, NIV). Jesus doesn't want you to carry your burdens alone. He is asking you to come to him for help.

"Two are better than one, because they have a good return for their labor: If either of them falls down, one can help the other up. But pity anyone who falls and has no one to help them up" (Ecclesiastes 4:9–10, NIV). Freeing yourself from domestic abuse is not done alone. Support from others is needed to succeed.

"So do not fear, for I am with you; do not be dismayed, for I am your God. I will strengthen you and help you; I will uphold you with my righteous right hand" (Isaiah 41:10, NIV). Do not fear speaking the truth. God says he is with you.

"God did not give us a spirit of timidity, but a spirit of power" (2 Timothy 1:7, NLT). God did not give you a spirit to be timid or fearful but a spirit of power to change your situation.

"The Lord is with me; I will not be afraid. What can man do to me?" (Psalm 118:6, NIV). Your abuser is not your god. He is not the controller of your life; God is. Take safety precautions if there is a possibility of death threats but remember God has more power over your life.

Hopelessness Versus Hope in God

Lesson 2

The purpose of this lesson is to help the abused woman recognize how learned helplessness has led to hopelessness. As a Christian, she needs hope in order to embark on the path to freeing herself from abuse.

As a victim of abuse, a woman may have learned helplessness, believing that nothing she does will change her situation—that she has no control over what is happening to her. In her book, *The Battered Woman*, Lenore E. Walker states, "People who feel helpless really believe that they have no influence over the success or failure of events that concern them." According to Walker, the battered woman does not believe anything she does will alter any outcome. The abused woman may think, "No matter what I do, I have no influence." ".... I am incapable and too stupid to learn how to change things."[2] This way of thinking was developed because she made multiple failed attempts to change her situation. This led to passivity, a sense of helplessness, hopelessness, and despair.

As she frees herself from the abuse, the woman must struggle to relearn hope. A woman who has recently left her abuser often is overwhelmed with immediate demands, such as providing for herself and her family, separation and divorce proceedings, custody battles, and the physical and psychological effects of the abuse on her and the children. It may seem unimaginable that she and her family will ever have a normal life.

God does not want his daughter to lose hope. Hope is essential in the life of every Christian. Webster defines hope as "to want or wish for something with a feeling of confident expectation." Hope comes with a confidence that what you hope for will happen.

For the woman who has experienced abuse, hope is absolutely essential to seeking change and healing. Hope allows her to move forward with a vision of a better, violence-free life for herself and her children. Regardless of all the suffering and loneliness she has experienced in the past, she must believe that her life can change and that she can receive joy and peace again.

Daring to Hope

Lamentations 3: 19-24
> The thought of my suffering and homelessness is bitter beyond words.
> I will never forget this awful time, as I grieve over my loss.
> Yet I still dare to hope when I remember this:
> The faithful love of the LORD never ends! His mercies never cease.
> Great is his faithfulness;
> his mercies begin afresh each morning.
> I say to myself, "The LORD is my inheritance;
>   therefore, I will hope in him!"

The writer in Lamentations states "… yet I still dare to hope…" after all the awful things that have happened to him.

The writer experiences a lot of suffering. (See Lamentations 3.) He experiences anguish and distress, he is called vile names and mocked, is forsaken by his people, and even feels God's wrath. Yet he has the courage to hope.

Similarly, the abused woman may have endured senseless physical and emotional violence, isolation, and total exhaustion. She may have felt unable to fight back or escape, abandoned by other people as well as God. But she, too, still can dare to hope.

Lamentations 3:19-21 states, "The thought of my suffering and homelessness is bitter beyond words. I will never forget this awful time, as I grieve over my loss. Yet I still dare to hope when I remember this." What motivates the speaker to continue to hope?

Verse 24 goes on to say, "The faithful love of the Lord never ends! His mercies never cease. Great is his faithfulness; his mercies begin afresh each morning. I say to myself, 'The Lord is my inheritance; therefore, I will hope in him!'"

The speaker decides to hope in God when he remembers God's unfailing love and grace, trusts in his faithfulness, and finds his self-worth in God. His gratitude for what God did for him in the past motivates him to return to God, the source of hope.

The abused Christian woman must remember and recognize the ways that God has blessed her. This will motivate her to put her hope in him, because he is faithful and will deliver her from the shame and pain of the abuse. It is important for her to examine the scriptures to regain her gratitude and trust in God. The scriptures demonstrate how many of God's people experienced oppression and suffering but were delivered when they cried out to the Lord. While God may not deliver her in the way that she imagined or expected, he does expect her to play her part in freeing herself.

For the woman who has left her abusive relationship, she must recognize that leaving itself is a triumph. God allowed her to leave. He set her free. There is hope for change in her freedom. Considering this fact alone can fill her with gratitude and hope.

As she moves ahead on the path of freedom and healing from the effects of domestic abuse, the woman has to hold onto God's promises. In Jeremiah 29:11, God says, "I know the plans I have for you… plans to prosper you and not to harm you, plans to give you hope and a future." The woman must place her confidence in that promise.

Self-Reflection
1. Read Lamentations 3, Proverbs 23:19, Psalm 24:3, and Romans 5:5. Write down your thoughts about each of these scriptures. What do these scriptures tell you about hope? How do they relate to the promise in Jeremiah 29:11?
2. Can you relate to learned helplessness? Did you try multiple times to do things that you thought would stop the abuse? When these actions failed, did you stop trying? Reflect on how you felt when these efforts failed. Bring those feelings to God.
3. Where is the source of your hope? If you feel as if you have no hope, what do you think will reawaken your hope?

4. Do you believe that your life can have joy and peace again? How will you achieve that goal?

Learning to Hope Again: Scriptures for Encouragement

"Why are you so downcast, O my soul? Why are you so disturbed within me? Put your hope in God, for I will yet praise him, my Savior and my God" (Psalm 42:5–6, NIV). Put your hope in God because he is your healer and shield.

"Be strong and take heart, all you who hope in the Lord" (Psalm 31:24, NIV). God wants you to hope in Him. He is the source of your joy. He is also your strength, protector, and healer.

"There is hope only for the living. For as they say, 'It is better to be a live dog than a dead lion'" (Ecclesiastes 9:4, NLT). There is always hope for the living. It does not make any difference if you live as a powerful lion or as a tame dog; being alive is what is important. A dead lion has no hope. The key is there is always hope in life.

"But blessed are those who trust in the Lord and have made the Lord their hope and confidence. They are like trees planted along a riverbank, with roots that reach deep into the water. Such trees are not bothered by the heat or worried by long months of drought. Their leaves stay green, and they never stop producing fruit" (Jeremiah 17:7–8, NLT). When you trust in God and put your hope in him, your spiritual roots will be strong, and you will be able to withstand any physical and emotional struggles as you seek change and healing.

"Do you not know? Have you not heard? The Lord is the everlasting God, the Creator of the ends of the earth. He will not grow tired or weary, and his understanding no one can fathom. He gives strength to the weary and increases the power of the weak. Even youth grow tired and weary, the young men stumble and fall; but those who hope in the Lord will renew their strength. They will soar on wings like eagles; they will run and not grow weary, they will walk and not be faint" (Isaiah 40:28–31, NIV). Don't grow tired and weary and lose hope for change! God doesn't! God will never lose hope in you. You may stumble and fall, grow weary, weak, old, and tired. Everyone does. But those who hope in the Lord, will find that he will renew their strength. Hope for a better tomorrow.

"Everything that was written in the past was written to teach us, so that through endurance and the encouragement of the Scriptures we might have hope" (Romans 15:4, NIV). The scriptures were written to give us hope for a better future. As a Christian woman, use these scriptures for encouragement and develop a conviction that your situation can change.

CHAPTER 6

IS THIS LOVE?

The abused woman must gain conviction that her definition of love needs to change. The experience of abuse has altered her view of love. The abused woman must carefully consider what love is and what love is not. She can learn to redefine love by considering how God loves. As she examines the scriptures and immerses herself in prayer, she will gain the conviction to replace her impaired view of love. Finally, when the abused woman reorganizes and embraces that the acceptance of God's love is needed before she can love him, herself, and others, she will then be able to love in the way that God desires.

Lesson 3

Most women marry because of what they believe to be love and enter the relationship with words and actions that express their definition of love. They also expect their partners to act in ways that meet their definition of love. Even in the case of the abused woman, during the dating period, her husband probably acted in ways that met her definition of love. For example, he might have been attentive and affectionate. He might have called her frequently just to say he loved her. Perhaps he took her to social events and for long walks in the park. During the dating period, he may even have listened to her suggestions and ideas when planning events. All these behaviors influenced her to marry him. She married because she believed he loved her.

As the abuse progresses in the relationship, the husband's actions seem increasingly unloving. This creates emotional turmoil in the woman. But, she loves her husband and wants her loving actions to be reciprocated. She may engage in different behaviors that she thinks will lead to loving actions on his part, but instead he becomes more unloving and abusive. In order to continue to believe that he loves her in spite of his abuse, she must alter her original definition of love. Over time, her perception of a loving husband is impaired. She no longer knows what healthy love is.

When the abused woman reflects on her relationship with her husband, she may realize that she was expecting to receive love from someone who didn't know what healthy love was and didn't know how to receive love or give it to others. As she gains more insight into her situation, she may also come to realize that not receiving reciprocal loving actions from her abuser may have affected her perception of God's love. She may feel that God doesn't love her, because he allowed the abuse. To move forward and receive her healing, she will have to change this damaged thinking.

God is love. To understand this love, the abused woman has to seek the source of love. God demonstrated what love is and how to love. As she learns more about God's love and accepts his love, the woman can learn to love herself and others the way that God intended. His love has the power to heal her damaged emotions.

What is love? The most beautiful definition of love is found in 1 Corinthians 13:4–8. We will apply this definition to an abusive relationship, as shown in the table below (which uses the New Living Translation of the verses).

What Love Is and What Love Is Not

Love is . . . *patient*.	Love allows for mistakes without criticizing everything you do. It doesn't focus on your mistakes to belittle you. It guides you patiently through difficulties by teaching you to master or overcome those difficulties.

Love is ... *kind.*	Love is empathic and compassionate. It produces goodness. It doesn't make you feel "stupid," "lazy," "ugly," like a "failure," "useless," or "unwanted." It does not ridicule you. It protects the weak and helpless. It always strives to bring comfort and joy, not fear and pain.
Love is ... *not jealous.*	Love is trusting, not suspicious. It does not spy on you or gather information to use against you. It does not stalk you. It does not try to alienate you from your friends and family. Love always expects the best and gives you the benefit of the doubt.
Love is ... *not boastful or proud.*	Love is humble. It does not need to be superior or make others feel like they are always wrong. Love listens and seeks input. It accepts responsibility rather than seeking to blame.
Love is ... *not rude.*	Love is respectful and considerate. It is not aggressive. It does not seek to degrade. Love does not ignore your presence or existence. Love acknowledges others and their needs.
Love ... *does not demand its own way.*	Love gives freedom. It does not demand, "my way or no way." It is not controlling! It respects your ability to make choices, even if they are sometimes wrong. Love accepts and rejoices in the individuality and uniqueness of others.

Love is ... *not irritable.*	Love is self-controlled. It is not easily angered, overly emotional, out of control, and does not experience "fits of rage." Love is calm and able to accept others' weaknesses or differences.
Love... *keeps no record of wrongs.*	Love is forgiving. It does not undermine or erode your confidence, keeping a record of mistakes. It does not hold grudges. Love moves forward, rather than focusing on the past.
Love ... *does not rejoice about injustice.*	Love embraces justice. It does not take away your moral and legal rights, which include the right to speak your mind, to share what is in your heart, or to participate in decision-making processes, as well as your right to privacy. It does not prohibit your right to socialize or have your own personal relationships. It does not view its own rights and needs as more important than the rights and needs of others. Love recognizes the value and equality of all people.
Love ... *rejoices when truth wins.*	Love cannot lie. It is not deceptive. Love does not keep secrets or twist reality. Rather, it rejoices when the truth is spoken. It does not deny abuse, but exposes it. Love is honest and open because it has nothing to hide.

Love ... *never loses faith.*	Love is faithful. It has faith in you and in your good character. It has faith in your capabilities and accomplishments. Love encourages you to have faith in yourself. Love always perseveres in doing right.
Love is ... *always hopeful.*	Love has high expectations for the future. It expects improvement and growth. Love seeks ultimate joy and peace for others.
Love ... *endures through every circumstance.*	Love does not change with the circumstances. It does not use bad circumstances or outside influences as an excuse for doing wrong or hurting someone. Love endures patiently to achieve what is right.
Love ... *will last forever.*	Love never dies. It does not reveal itself only when everything is going well. It does not disappear during disagreements or conflicts. Love lasts forever.

The definition of love in 1 Corinthians proves that an abused woman is not truly loved by her husband. What she might have believed was love wasn't love at all. It is important that she recall her definition of love before she entered into the abusive relationship and see how that definition has been impaired by the abuse. She will have to replace that impaired view of love with the scriptural definition of love as God intended.

In his article, "What Is Healthy Love," Jef Gazley describes a healthy love relationship as characterized by individuality. Each partner brings out the best qualities in the other. Each one also encourages self-sufficiency and growth in the other and accepts the limitations of oneself and the other. Both partners are open to individual change, as well as to change in the relationship. Physical, intellectual, emotional, and spiritual intimacy exist along with freedom to honestly ask for what they want. Both partners are able to give and receive without attempting to control or change the other person. Each partner has high self-esteem and is able to accept commitment. Either partner can enjoy solitude as well as spontaneous expressions of feelings. Each individual also is able to care for the other without feeling responsible for him or her.

Importantly, Mr. Gazley emphasizes that healthy relationships are not characterized by unconditional love. Unconditional love characterizes the feeling of a parent toward a child because most parents love their children regardless of behavior. Adults demand to be treated with dignity in order to stay in the relationship.[1]

Self-Reflection

Go back and read Chapter 1, "The Marriage," for self-reflection as you consider the questions below:

1. What was your definition of love before your marriage? List words and actions that you associated with love back then.
2. Compare that list to the words and actions you have experienced in your relationship.
3. Have you compromised your standard for a loving relationship over time? If so, list the effects of this compromise on your own feelings and behaviors. For example, do you experience a sense of failure, rejection, or inadequacy?
4. Are you or were you "performing tasks" to earn his love?
5. If so, what did you do? How did you feel as a result? For example, did you feel angry that he was never pleased with or did not acknowledge what you did? Or, did you become emotionally numb as the result of his constant demands?
6. What did he do to make you afraid? Do you associate those behaviors with love? Can behaviors that create fear be considered loving? Can a person truly love you when you feel unsafe around him?
7. Have you ever questioned your ability to give or receive love? What influences this self-doubt?
8. Read 1 Peter 4:8b. It states, "Love covers over a multitude of sins." What does that mean to you? Remember that compromising the emotional and physical safety of your children is not a demonstration of love.

9. Read 1 Corinthians 13:4–8 and apply that definition of love to your relationship. Write down your thoughts. What you might have believed was love wasn't love at all. To move forward as you seek healing, you will have to get rid of your old way of thinking and learn how to experience love as it is revealed in the scriptures. Learn how to love yourself first, and then you can learn to love others (Matthew 22:39).

Self-Love: Scriptures for Encouragement

(Self-love, as explained by 1 Corinthians 13:4–8)

Love is … *patient*.	Be patient with yourself. You will make mistakes as you move forward in God's love. Change, but remember it does not occur instantly.
Love is … *kind*.	Be kind and compassionate toward yourself. Be kind to yourself by resting, exercising, or participating in fitness activities, and eating a healthy diet. Do activities that will lead to self-respect. Find your talents or gifts, for example, art, dance, or singing, and develop them. Make learning a continual process to sharpen your mind and increase your knowledge by reading books or attending classes.
Love is … *not jealous*.	Do not waste precious time and energy envying others. Be content with and grateful for what God has given you.

Love is ... *not boastful or proud.*	Do not worry about what others think about you. Let go of the idea of the perfect family and woman. Consider what is really important to you and pursue that. Be open about your imperfections and weaknesses and seek advice.
Love is ... *not rude.*	Protect your rights and dignity while also respecting others' rights and dignity. Expect others to consider you and your children's feelings and opinions. Remember that all people, including you and your children, deserve full respect.
Love does ... *not demand its own way.*	Determine your personal convictions and calmly share them. Also, listen to others' opinions and ideas and be open to input so that you can grow.
Love is ... *is not irritable.*	Do not let the emotional state of others control you. Be aware of negative messages about yourself—you are stupid or not good enough. Pay attention to your thoughts to see if they reflect someone else's negative comments about you. God has given you a powerful tool called "choice" to challenge negative thoughts and replace them with his truths.

Love does ... *not keep records when it has been wronged.*	Let go of the "whys," "what ifs," "should haves," or "if onlys." Holding on to these negative thoughts will keep you locked into bitterness and disappointments. You start your process of healing when you forgive others and yourself. Remember that God has forgiven you.
Love is ... *never glad about injustices.*	Never, ever compromise your moral and legal rights. Embrace justice for yourself and others. You may want to look for opportunities to seek justice for other abused women.
Love rejoices ... *when truth wins.*	Speak the truth in love. Expose abuse for what it is.
Love never ... *loses faith.*	Don't lose faith in yourself or God. God has faith in your capabilities, goals, and dreams. Part of God's plan is for you to succeed in life.
Love is ... *always hopeful.*	Always hope for positive change. Hope for peace, happiness, and a brighter tomorrow.
Love ... *endures through every circumstance.*	Remember that you are a survivor and conqueror. You have incredible strength, as evidenced by your victory over abuse. You are empowered by God's love to endure every difficulty.
Love will ... *last forever.*	Do not give up on God's love. His love lasts forever.

God Is Love

Lesson 4

The Bible tells us "God is love." Not only is God love, he is the source of love as stated by John: "Dear friends, let us continue to love one another for love comes from God.

Everyone who loves has been born of God and knows God. Whoever does not love does not know God, because God is love" (1 John 4:7–8, NIV). The source of love for the Christian woman is God. Her husband cannot completely fulfill her need for love.

God's Love

God is filled with grace and compassion and he loves unconditionally. His love is unfailing (Psalm 86:15) and it lasts forever (Psalm 100:5). However, his love does not compromise.

Deuteronomy 6:5 commands, "And you must love the Lord your God with all your heart, all your soul, and all your strength." God wants all of the woman's love, not a small portion. When her abusive relationship consumes every area of her life, it leaves little room for God. God wants her relationship with him to take priority over all other relationships.

All Christians show their love for God by obeying his commands (1 John 2:5). This means that following God's Word and doing as it says is more important than obeying the word of any human being, including her husband. For example, if a wife hides her husband's abusive actions through deceit, she is compromising God's commands in favor of her husband's expectations.

Placing God's commands above all other commands comes with a wonderful promise from Jesus, "If you hold to my teaching, you are really my disciples. Then you will know the truth, and the truth will set you free" (John 8:31–32, NIV).

In God's love there is no fear. His love has power over all fears. When a woman lives in God's love, her love "…has no fear, because perfect love expels all fear" (1 John 4:18, NLT). If she is afraid it is because of the uncertainty of the future and God's judgment, which shows that she does not fully understand his love. God's love can resolve her fears even when she feels he is punishing her. God's discipline produces good outcome in her life. Accepting abuse does not produce a good outcome. It destroys her spirit and creates paralyzing fear.

God's love involves accountability. God sent prophets and even his Son to warn people about the consequences of drifting from his love and failing to change. When the people repeatedly fail to change their sinful behaviors, they have to suffer the consequences of their actions:

> The Lord, the Lord, the compassionate and gracious God, slow to anger, abounding in love and faithfulness, maintaining love to thousands, and forgiving wickedness, rebellion and sin. Yet he does not leave the guilty unpunished; he punishes the children and their children for the sin of the parents to the third and fourth generation. (Exodus 34:6–7, NIV)

For the abused woman, loving her husband means exposing the abuse and seeking accountability. If she does not do this, the family will have to face the consequences of the abuse from generation to generation. But the good news is that, if she loves God and follows his commands, he will keep his "…covenant of love to a thousand generations." (Deuteronomy 7:9, NIV). Like all good parents, God's love involves accountability to help Christians change sinful behaviors. Jesus states, "Those whom I love I rebuke and discipline. So be earnest, and repent" (Revelation 3:19, NIV). God disciplines the ones he loves. The goal of his discipline is to give a woman hope, confidence, courage, peace, and validation that he is looking out for her.

Even though God is slow to anger and he gives an abundance of grace and love, he also expects the abused Christian woman to change behaviors that may damage her physical and spiritual life. Jesus promises, "I have come that they may have life, and have it to full" (John 10:10, NIV). Not only does Jesus want her to live, he wants her to enjoy the fullness of life. Acceptance of abuse and not seeking accountability stops her from enjoying the fullness of life Jesus promises. As the woman repents by being obedient to God's commands, she will gain a better understanding of God's love.

Although changing sinful behaviors allows the abused Christian woman to live in God's love, she does not have to earn this love. Unlike the abusive husband, God does not offer performance-based love. Instead—

> God showed how much he loves us by sending his only son into the world that we might have eternal life through him. This is real love. It is not that we loved God, but that he loved us and sent his son as a sacrifice to take away our sins. (1 John 4:9–10, NLT)

> But God showed his great love for us by sending Christ to die for us while we were still sinners. (Romans 5:8, NLT)

God loves the abused woman when she is disobedient, and isn't "good enough," with all her imperfections. He loves her not because of what she can do or has done for him, but because his love is unconditional.

Romans 13:10 (NLT) further states, "Love does no wrong to others, so love fulfills the requirement of God's law." God's law of love replaces all other laws. His love does not cause or justify abuse. It does not threaten a woman's safety or the safety of her children. In God's love, there is always a sense of trust, safety, and protection. God loves her so much and he wants her to put her trust in his love (1 John 4:16). The abused Christian woman should not be afraid to put her trust in God's love. He wants her to learn to trust him as a father, husband, and Lord. Unlike an abusive husband, he will not be harsh, misuse her, or betray her trust.

God is the source of love. His love does not compromise or produce fear, and it requires accountability. Most importantly, it does not depend on a woman's performance or ability to earn his love. In order to heal, the abused woman must accept God's love and be filled with his love before she can love herself and love others.

Self-Reflection

Read the scriptures below for each section. Write down your thoughts and consider the following questions:

God Is Love. Read Psalm 86:15, Psalm 100:5, 1 John 4:8b, 1 John 4:7 and write your thoughts.

- When you consider that your source of love is God and not your partner, how does that make you feel?
- The scripture is clear that anyone who does not love is not of God. That means anyone who habitually inflicts violence on others, whether physical or psychological, is not of God. Can you accept this statement? Or do you feel that there are exceptions?

God's Love

1. **God's love does not compromise.** Read Deuteronomy 6:5, Matthew 10:37, and 1 John 2:5. Write down your thoughts.
   - If your husband asked you to lie about his abusive behaviors, what would you do? What would influence your choice?

2. *In God's love there is no fear.* Read 1 John 4:18, Romans 13:10, and 1 John 4:16. Write down your thoughts.
   - Do you believe that your husband consciously chooses to love you, but unconsciously hurts you?
   - Can a person who makes you feel unsafe be the same person who loves you deeply?
   - Are you afraid of God because of his judgment? Pray that his love will help you resolve your fears.

3. *There is accountability in God's love.* Read Exodus 34:6–7, Revelation 3:19, Deuteronomy 7:9, and John 10:10. Again, write down your thoughts.
   - Do you cover up your children's sins because you don't want them to face the consequences? If so, why? If not, why not?
   - Are you demonstrating love by covering up abuse?
   - How do you feel when you read the scripture that says, "He punishes the children and their children for the sin of the parents to the third and fourth generation"? The good news is that when you repent, he keeps his covenant of steadfast love "to a thousand generations."

4. *God's love does not require performance.* Read 1 John 4:9–10 and Romans 5:8 and write down your thoughts.
- Do you think you can earn God's love?
- God loves you, regardless of your performance. How do you feel, knowing that God's love cannot be earned by actions?
- Do you trust God's love? He wants you to put your trust in his love. Recall what he has already done for you to help build your faith and strengthen your trust in him.

God's Unchanging Love: Scriptures for Encouragement

"How priceless is your unfailing love, O God! People take refuge in the shadow of your wings" (Psalm 36:7, NIV). Find protection from your abuse in the shadow of God's wings. His love for you never changes!

"Because of the Lord's great love we are not consumed, for his compassions never fail" (Lamentations 3:22, *NIV*). God is filled with compassion and willing to forgive your many sins because of his love for you.

"I love those who love me, and those who seek me diligently find me" (Proverbs 8:17, ESV). God loves you and wants you to have the desire to know him more.

"And this is what will happen: When you, on your part, will obey these directives, keeping and following them, God, on his part, will keep the covenant of loyal love that he made with your ancestors: He will love you, he will bless you, he will increase you" (Deuteronomy 7:12–13, *The Message*). When you have done your part and stop the abuse and continue to be obedient to God, he will love and bless your life to the full.

"For the Lord God is our sun and our shield. He gives us grace and glory. The Lord will withhold no good thing from those who do what is right" (Psalm 84:11, NLT). God is your shield and protector. He loves you and gives you grace so that you can change and reflect his glory. He is not going to withhold what you need to break free from domestic abuse if you do what is right.

"And we know that in all things God works for the good of those who love him who have been called according to his purpose" (Romans 8:28, NIV). God always works for the good for those who are in his family. He has a purpose for your life. Don't let the effects of the abuse stop you from living your purpose.

Embracing God's Love

Lesson 5

Every human is made in God's image. In Genesis 1:26 (NIV) God says, "Let us make human beings in our image, to be like us." Knowing that the abused woman is made in God's image should be the basis of her self-worth. As Paul states, "You have put on the new self, which is being renewed in knowledge in the image of its Creator" (Colossians 3:10, NIV). When the woman chooses to follow Christ, she becomes a new person who is more like the God who created her. Paul adds, "Don't you realize that your body is the temple of the Holy Spirit, who lives in you and was given to you by God? You do not belong to yourself" (1 Corinthians 6:19, NLT). God made the Christian woman so that he can live in her. She is God's holy temple. Anyone who violates her body violates God's temple; abuse destroys that temple.

God's motive for creating the Christian woman was love. "Even before he made the world, God loved us and chose us in Christ to be holy and without fault in his eyes" (Ephesians 1:4, NLT). God loves the woman with all her faults. In fact, his love overpowers her faults.

Before she was born he chose her to be part of his family through Jesus Christ (Ephesians 1:5–6). He did this because he loved her, and it gives him great pleasure and joy. When the abused woman starts to blame herself for the failure of the relationship, she can find comfort in the fact that God sees her as blameless in his sight. Regardless of how she sees herself, God is willing to lavish his love on her, because she is his "beloved daughter" (1 John 3:1). Nothing she did during her abusive relationship will ever stop God from loving her.

Each Christian is the focus of God's love, the most valuable of all his creations. The abused Christian woman is God's prized possession: In his goodness, he chose to make his own children by giving us his true Word. And she, out of all creation, became his choice possession (James 1:18). Her mother may have given birth to her but God planned her existence. He took care her of her in the darkness of her mother's womb.

He saw her little hands, and feet, and full body developed even before she was born (Psalm 139:15–16). God was there from the beginning and has set her apart, as he states: "Before I formed you in the womb I knew you, before you were born I set you apart" (Jeremiah 1:5, NIV).

Not only did God care for the woman in her mother's womb, he has cared for her since her birth. God says, "I have cared for you since you were born. Yes, I carried you before you were born. I will be your God throughout your lifetime—until your hair is white with age. I made you, and I will care for you. I will carry you along and save you" (Isaiah 46:3–4, NLT). What a comforting thought. He promises to care for the woman during her entire lifetime. He took care of her during her abuse, when she might have felt he wasn't there. And he is always with her, delights in her, and has the power to save her from abuse. He will quiet her anxious and fearful heart with his love and rejoice over her with singing (Zephaniah 3:17). And, he also wants to be her husband and Redeemer (Isaiah 54:5). He brought her out of the humiliation and embarrassment of her abuse, and like an abandoned wife devastated with grief, he welcome her back into his arms.

Jesus confirms the woman's worth: "Are not two sparrows sold for a penny? Yet not one of them will fall to the ground apart from the will of your father. And even the very hairs of your head are numbered. So don't be afraid; you are worth more than many sparrows" (Matthew 10:29–31, NIV). His love is the basis for her self-worth. When the woman feels that her value has been diminished by her abuse, the scriptures remind her that she is one of God's valuable creations.

God's love for his Christian daughter is demonstrated through Christ's life and death. She can state: "It is no longer I who live, but Christ lives in me. So I live my life in this earthly body by trusting in the Son of God, who loved me and gave himself for me" (Galatians 2:20, NLT).

God also demonstrated his love through the gift of his Holy Spirit, through which "we know how dearly God loves us, because he has given us the Holy Spirit to fill our hearts with his love" (Romans 5:5, NLT). Not only does God love his Christian daughter, but he also wants her to experience his love through an emotional connection, such as feeling his love through her senses. To accomplish this emotional connection, God sent his Holy Spirit to fill her heart with his love. The

Holy Spirit allows the woman to experience God's presence similar to the way she experiences the presence of a person she loves. For example, the Spirit allows her to feel happy and safe, as if God were at her side when she talks to him in her prayers and meditation. God wants his daughter to call him "Father," so he pours his Holy Spirit into her to prompt her to recognize him (Galatians 4:6). When feeling sad and alone, she can come into God's presence and let his love fill her heart with joy and peace.

God wants the abused Christian woman to put her hope in his unfailing love: The Lord "takes pleasure in those who honor him, in those who trust in his constant love." (Psalm 147:11, GNT). The abused woman should put her hope and trust in his love because it never fails. His love and compassion last forever. (Psalm 25:6) She can find refuge in his unfailing love (Psalm 36:7). Jesus says, "I have loved you even as the Father has loved me. Remain in my love" (John 15:9, NLT). The abused Christian woman must hold on to God's unfailing love. His love has the power to heal her from the effects of her abuse.

Once a woman accepts, experiences, and embraces God's love, she can learn how to truly love God and, in turn, love herself and others. The Christian woman's most important goal is to love God. Proverbs 8:17 says "I love all who love me. Those who search will surely find me" (NLT). Jesus also wants the woman to love his Father. Jesus commands her to "… love the Lord your God with all your heart, all your soul, and all your mind" (Matthew 22:37, NIV).

An authentic love for God is expressed by living out God's commands. Jesus said, "The person who knows my commandments and keeps them, that's who loves me. And the person who loves me will be loved by my Father, and I will love him and make myself plain to him" (John 14:21). Jesus plainly states, "If you love my Father I will love and make myself known to you."

How does the woman remain in God's love? By doing what Jesus said in John 15:10—"When you obey me, you remain in my love, just as I obey my Father and remain in his love." She must not let the experience of domestic violence stop her from obeying God's commands. She has to speak the truth and seek change to experience a genuine relationship with God.

Loving God does not require a woman to sacrifice her life and the lives of her children by continuing to live in an abusive relationship. God wants a loving response that comes from the heart, however, not sacrifices. Loving God "… with all your heart, with all your understanding, and with your strength … is more important than all burnt offerings and sacrifices" (Mark 12:33, NIV).

As the Christian woman grows in an authentic, loving relationship with her God, she will be filled with his love. This love will enable her to understand and give love to others. She also will be able to experience an all-encompassing love of God her Father.

It will help the abused Christian woman to grow in her love for God by understanding his mercy toward her. Jesus says, "But go and learn what this means. 'I desire mercy, not sacrifice.' For I have not come to call the righteous, but sinners" (Matthew 9:13, NIV). God loves the abused Christian woman with all her faults and mistakes and she must learn to love herself in the same way. God's love is kind, compassionate, gentle, patient, and filled with grace and mercy.

The woman therefore can be kind, gentle, and patient with herself. God's love should allow her to forgive herself for tolerating the abuse and help her to discard the "what ifs," "whys," and "if onlys" in her mind.

The Christian woman also needs to understand that loving herself is necessary in order to obey God's most important commands:

> For the commandments say, "You must not commit adultery. You must not murder. You must not steal. You must not covet." These and other such commandments are summed up in this one commandment: "Love your neighbor as yourself." (Romans 13:9, NLT)

In this scripture and in Matthew 22:37–38, Jesus is indicating that loving your neighbor as yourself is just as important as loving God with all your heart, soul, and mind. But if a woman does not love herself, how can she love her neighbor in the same way?

When a Christian wife develops a solid understanding of God's love, she will expect to be valued and loved as Paul commands: "Husbands, love your wives just as Christ loved the church and gave himself up for her to make her holy, cleansing her by washing with water through the word, and present her to himself as a radiant church, without stain or wrinkle or any other blemish, but holy and blameless. In the same way, husbands ought to love their wives as their own bodies. He who loves his wife loves himself" (Ephesians 5:25–28, NIV). God wants his daughter to be loved the way Jesus loves the church.

The scriptures make it clear that loving God and oneself allows the Christian woman to love others. And loving others is not optional. In John 15:17, Jesus commands Christians to "love each other." He elaborates: "Love each other as I have loved you" (John 15:12, NIV). The abused Christian woman must love others in the same way Jesus loves her. In 1 John 4:19 we find that "...we love each other because he loved us first" (NLT). Understanding Jesus' love allows her to love others. John the apostle states, "Dear friends, since God loved us that much, we surely ought to love each other. No one has ever seen God, but if we love each other, God lives in us, and his love has been brought to full expression in us" (1 John 4:11–12, NLT). God's love is pure; it is not coerced, manipulated, or perverted. It does not cause guilt or confusion. It is not deceptive. The woman reveals God to others by loving them with the love that God has given her.

The abused Christian woman, however, may struggle in understanding what it means to love her abuser. In loving her abuser, the Christian woman must carefully consider what it means to love as God loved. Loving her abuser does not mean accepting abusive actions. God's love involves accountability. Her love for the abuser should motivate her to expose the abuse and seek help. Tolerating the abuse helps no one, including the abuser.

God also wants his daughter to love others with a clear conscience. Paul states, "The purpose of my instructions is that all believers would be filled with love that comes from a pure heart, a clear conscience, and genuine faith" (1 Timothy 1:5, NLT). The abused Christian woman must pay close attention to her conscience. When she feels that something has violated her conscience, she must recognize that it is not of God.

Conclusion

Each woman is made in God's image and his motive for creating her was love. She is the focus of his love. God wants the abused Christian woman to have a connection to his love, which is expressed in Jesus' final sacrifice on the cross for her sins. No further sacrifice is required on her part.

According to Jesus' definition of love, she also must love herself before she can love others. She should not be confused about how she should love or be loved in a relationship. In addition, she is commanded to love others with a clear conscience. God's Word and Spirit will teach her how to give and receive love.

Finally, the abused Christian woman must remember that nothing can separate her from God's love. As Paul puts it:

> Who shall separate us from the love of Christ? Shall trouble or hardship or persecution or famine or nakedness or danger or sword? As it is written: "For your sake we face death all day long; we are considered as sheep to be slaughtered." No, in all these things we are more than conquerors through him who loved us. (Roman 8:35–37, NIV)

Regardless of the hardship she endured, God loves her. A woman who has endured abuse can find comfort in the fact that nothing she did or has experienced has the power to separate her from God's love.

I pray for you as Paul did:

> That out of his glorious riches he may strengthen you with power through his Spirit in your inner being, so that Christ may dwell in your hearts through faith. And I pray that you, being rooted and established in love, may have power, together with all the saints, to grasp how wide and long and high and deep is the love of Christ, and to know this love that surpasses knowledge—that you may be filled to the measure of all the fullness of God. (Ephesians 3:16–19, NIV)

Put your hope and trust in God's love. Let your roots grow deeper in his marvelous love, so you will be filled with the power that comes only from God. This power allows you to discard all your dysfunctional ways of loving and to love as he intended.

Self-Reflection

Read the scriptures below for each section. Write down your thoughts and consider the following questions:

1. *You are made in God's image.* Read Genesis 1:26, Colossians 3:10, and 1 Corinthians 6:19. Write down your thoughts.
   - What behaviors did you engage in as part of an abusive relationship that has affected your self-worth?
   - How does knowing that you are a reflection of God's image influence your self-worth? Embrace this image. You put on a new self when you accepted Christ as your Savior.
   - Which is easier, knowing God loves you, or accepting God's love? How is your answer influenced by your past?
   - What life experiences have influenced your answers in this section?
   - How has your abuse hindered you from being able to accept God's love?
   - Your mind and your body are God's holy temple. How does knowing that make you feel? How does abuse affect God's temple?

2. *God's motive for creating you was his love.* Read Ephesians 1:4–6 and write down your thoughts.
   - Does it seem that you are at fault for everything? List your faults. Ephesians 1:4 states that you are holy and without fault in God's eyes. Can you accept this statement without self-criticism? List your strengths. Use them to overpower your weaknesses.
   - God knew self-acceptance would be difficult, so he extended his grace to you. Can you accept God's grace? Or, do you feel you don't deserve it? Pray for the Holy Spirit to help you gain understanding and acceptance of his grace.

3. *You are the focus of God's love, the most valuable of all his creations.* Read James 1:18, Psalm 139:15–16, Isaiah 46:3–4, Zephaniah 3:17, and Matthew 10:29–31, and write down your thoughts.
   - How do you feel when you read that you are God's most "valuable" and "priceless" possession?
   - Do you think others have more value than you do? If you do have that belief, why?
   - How has the value you placed on yourself played a role in your acceptance of abuse?
   - When you call God "Father," how does that make you feel?
   - What was your relationship with your earthly father like? What images come to mind when you recall your earthly father? Can you imagine being lovingly cared for by an earthly father? Why or why not? Your interactions with your earthly father will influence how you see God as a father.
   - How does the awareness that God not only planned your birth but also looked forward to your arrival affect the way you see yourself?
   - Can you list past events in your life that reveal God caring for you?
   - Do you see God as your Father today? Do you believe that he is taking care of your needs and that he loves you? Explain. It may be difficult to accept that God was there during the abuse and did not stop the abuse. To overcome that difficulty, focus on the little things he did, for example, strengthening you physically to endure the abuse or sending a friend to help you with childcare to fill your heart with gratitude, which validates his presence.

4. *God has demonstrated his love for you by his Son's life and death and also by the gift of the Holy Spirit.* Read 1 John 5:9, Galatians 2:20, Romans 5:5b, and Galatians 4:6, and write down your thoughts.
   - What does "He has given his Holy Spirit to fill our hearts with his love" mean to you?
   - How are you emotionally connected to God's love? What emotions do you experience when in God's presence? For example, do you feel safe and happy in God's presence? If you

feel anger, self-doubt, or a lack of trust in God, ask his Holy Spirit to help you replace those emotions with joy, peace, and a sense of safety.

5. *God wants you to put your hope in his unfailing love.* Read Psalm 147:11, Psalm 25:6, and 1 John 3:1, and write down your thoughts.
   - What does "hope" and "unfailing" mean? According to Webster's dictionary, *hope* means "to desire with expectation of fulfillment." *Unfailing* is defined as steadfast; *steadfast* is defined as faithful or determined; *faithful* is defined as confident and trusting.
   - Do you desire and expect God's love every minute of your day?
   - Do you have confidence and trust in his love? Pray and ask God to help you put your confidence in his love, because it has the power to free you from the effects of your abuse.

6. *God wants the abused woman to love Him.* Read Proverbs 8:17 and Matthew 22:37, and write down your thoughts.
   - How do you love God? List your actions that reflect your love for him.

7. *God wants the abused woman to love herself before she can love others.* Read Romans 12:9 and Matthew 22:39, and write down your thoughts.
   - Do you have trouble loving yourself? If so, why?
   - How do you demonstrate that you love yourself?
   - When you reflect on your abuse, how do you feel about yourself? Pray and use God's love to forgive yourself.
   - What "whys," "what ifs," and "if onlys" continue to cross your mind? If you continue to dwell on these questions, use God's love to free yourself.

8. *God shows how a woman should be loved in a relationship.* Read Ephesians 5:25–28 and write down your thoughts.
   - How do you visualize your partner or future partner loving you? How does your vision align with this scripture?

9. *God wants you to love others because he first loved you.* Read 1 John 4:19, John 15:12, and John 4:11–12, and write down your thoughts.
    - How can you love others without acknowledging and accepting God's love first?
    - Why do you love others? How does God's love influence your love for others?
    - What does "God lives in us and his love has been brought to full expression through us" mean? How did your love for your husband play a role in your acceptance of his abuse?
    - Do you think that exposing the abuse is a reflection of love? If not, why not?

10. *God wants you to love others with a clear conscience.* Read 1 Timothy 1:5 and write down your thoughts.
    - What does loving people with a clear conscience mean to you?

Live in God's Love: Scriptures for Encouragement

What marvelous love the Father has extended to us! Just look at it—we're called children of God! That's who we really are. But that's also why the world doesn't recognize us or take us seriously, because it has no idea who he is or what he's up to. (1 John 3:1, *The Message*)

No matter what your earthly mother and father did—you might not have felt loved or might have felt rejected by them—your heavenly family accepts you and will not reject you. You were accepted in this new family when you decided to choose Christ as your Savior. In this family you are called "the daughter of God"!

"Many waters cannot quench love; rivers cannot sweep it away. If one were to give all the wealth of one's house for love, it would be utterly scorned" (Song of Songs 8:7, NIV). God loves you deeply and his love cannot be washed away by rivers, nor is any amount of money enough to buy that love. Hold on to that thought!

"Therefore, as God's chosen people, holy and dearly loved, clothe yourselves with compassion, kindness, humility, gentleness and patience. Bear with each other and forgive one another if any of you has a grievance against someone. Forgive as the Lord forgave you. And over all these virtues put on love, which binds them all together in perfect unity" (Colossians 3:12–14, NIV). Love is the glue that binds us together. Seek it; use it to forgive yourself and others. Always incorporate his love into your daily life, because it has the power to change you and heal your damaged emotions.

"May the grace of the Lord Jesus Christ, and the love of God, and the fellowship of the Holy Spirit be with you all" (2 Corinthians 13:14, NIV). May God's grace and love and his Holy Spirit be with you as you free yourself from the effects of domestic abuse.

"Give all your worries and cares to God, for he cares about you" (1 Peter 5:7, NLT). Give to God all your worries, fears, uncertainties of life, and weakness, because he cares for you. He will work out things for your good.

"For the word of the Lord holds true, and we can trust everything he does" (Psalm 33:4, NLT). Trust in the Word of God as you seek healing. It has the power to free you.

CHAPTER 7

DOING THE WORK: ANGER, FORGIVENESS, AND GRIEVING

To heal, it is critical for the abused Christian woman to get in touch with her anger and to find healthy ways to express and manage it. She must gain a new understanding of forgiveness and use that knowledge to forgive others and herself. The woman also needs to realize that grieving is part of the process of healing from an abusive relationship. Grieving this type of relationship involves much more the grieving of losses associated with separation or divorce. The abused woman may find herself grieving the loss of her hopes and dreams for a happy relationship long before she ever considers separation.

 **EDITH**

I REMEMBER DRIVING down a major highway one hot afternoon with no end destination, with the desire to clear my mind. My brain was in overload and I needed to let go of old memories before I could add any new information.

For the first time in the relationship my anger was coming to the surface. I was very good at suppressing and internalizing my anger. I had learned to fear confrontation when I felt mistreated by others. This fear was instilled in the depth of my psyche due to childhood experiences. During my childhood and teen years, I was often teased at school. Since I wasn't physically strong to fight back, I limited my participation in games and team activities that might lead to altercations. My way of coping was to observe my peers play from a distance to prevent the chance of being the scapegoat.

I brought that same fear of confrontation into my marital relationship. I was afraid to disagree due to the fear of getting physically or emotionally harmed. For example, there was an incident where I disagreed with the idea of applying for a loan to pay some of our debts. I believed getting a loan would have had an adverse effect on our credit. When I verbalized my reason for disagreeing, my husband became argumentative. To decrease the possibility of the communication escalating into violence, I gave in and agreed to apply for the loan. I also behaved like I was resolved with the decision, but the truth was, internally I was steaming with anger because I felt manipulated to concede. This way of dealing with disagreement was evident in all areas of our relationship, from finances to household decisions, such as what types of food to buy for the family or types of furniture or appliances for the house. The pattern was that my input was disregarded and I felt coerced into agreeing to what he desired, and then I stuffed my angry feelings.

A key stimulus that activated my suppressed anger to come into full steam was when I found out that my husband had had an affair. To complicate things, the woman called my house to validate the affair. I was furious! It wasn't the affair itself that fueled the explosion of my anger, but the fact that my husband allowed the woman to disrespect me by calling my home. That anger led me to take control of my finances and others areas of my life. I stopped contributing to the joint account and paid my share of the bills based on my income. I was tired of being deceptive about what was happening at home and was going to speak to anyone who was willing to listen. I was tired of giving in to financial decisions that didn't make sense and that had a negative effect on our income. I refused to sign any new loan application. If he hit me again, I was going to press charges. I became angry with myself for letting my fears stop me from setting boundaries, such as the ability to say no and not compromise when I didn't agree with him. I decided if I didn't agree with a decision and my moral conscience was clear before God, I wasn't going to give in.

When I started making these changes, I began to take control of my life. Even though I was beginning to feel like I was in control, my anger was seeping into other areas of my life. My kids were becoming the recipients. Any sense of disrespect in their tone of voice or actions would send me into a fit of rage. At work, I was overly sensitive when I felt my voice wasn't heard or my coworkers were talking about me behind my back or were dishonest. I overreacted when I felt I was being deceived or lied to and when those in charge, especially men, used harsh or controlling voice to lead.

As I drove that day, I came to recognize that even though my anger had motivated me to take some control in the relationship, it was changing me into a person I didn't like. I was becoming resentful and bitter. It took too much emotional energy to be angry. I needed to do something to control my anger. If I didn't find ways to control my anger, it was going to damage my relationship with others and most importantly my relationship with God. I needed to do something drastic and I needed to do it now!

Dealing with Anger and Conflict

Anger is one of the most common human emotions. Anger is defined as "a strong feeling of displeasure and (usually) of antagonism."[1] We humans become angry because "psychological or physical boundaries are being crossed against our wishes; our children, family, community or selves are threatened with harm; needs are not met for human dignity, respect of rights, or justice."[2]

When we become angry for these reasons, we need to do something. Jesus got angry, and here is what he did:

> In the temple courts he found men selling cattle, sheep, and doves, and others sitting at tables exchanging money. So he made a whip out of cords, and drove all from the temple area, both sheep and cattle; he scattered the coins of the moneychangers

and overturned their tables. To those who sold doves he said, "Get these out of here! How dare you turn my father's house into a market!" (John 2:14–16, NIV)

They were using God's place of worship for business, which affected others who came to worship. Jesus used a radical approach to get the people out of the temple.

There are many legitimate reasons why the abused woman will be angry. One of the reasons is the inability to fight back as she is physically and emotionally assaulted. She may feel helpless and incapable of protecting herself, which leads to frustration. She also may feel anger because she is not able to express her feelings and believes that she has to pretend everything is OK in the relationship. She is bound to feel anger toward her abuser for a variety of reasons. She may be angry that he has destroyed the family financially and/or failed to assist with childcare and housework. She may have anger about the emotional and physical suffering he has inflicted upon the children and her. In addition, she may be angry with God for allowing the abuse. She may be angry with others for not believing her story, not offering support, or for giving advice that was ineffective or harmful. Finally, she may be angry with herself for allowing fear and shame to paralyze her and for exposing herself and her children to prolonged physical and emotional abuse.

Anger is energy. When a woman suppresses or denies the energy of her anger, it will be internalized. Internalizing anger may lead to physical and mental illnesses like depression and anxiety.[3] Internalized anger is also linked to drug and alcohol abuse and possibly addiction in general, which may be used to block the emotional pain beneath the anger.[4] A woman's suppressed anger also can be misdirected toward the innocent, often children or pets. The woman may not be in touch with her anger while she is in the abusive relationship. When she begins to open up about her abuse and recognizes what has occurred in her relationship, the suppressed anger will resurface.

There are many reasons why she suppresses or denies her anger. She may have learned to suppress her anger in the relationship due to the fear of provoking more abuse. The woman also may deny her anger as a way of coping with the abuse. In addition, she may have learned to bury her anger as a child. If she did not learn effective ways of expressing anger as a child, she will have extreme difficulty in dealing with the anger that results from abuse. Regardless of her earlier patterns of dealing with anger, the abused woman usually experiences some fear that if she allows herself to get in touch with her anger, it might lead to a loss of control and violent actions.[5]

To heal, the abused woman must get in touch with her anger. She must learn appropriate ways to express that anger to move forward in the healing process. Holding on to anger until it becomes unbearable may lead to an eruption in which the woman loses control and becomes violent herself. Pamela Cooper-White explains, "There is a difference between expressing anger and using violence. Anger can be expressed nonviolently."[6]

Anger can be an important tool for change. Anger can stimulate a woman to seek justice and accountability. The abused woman has the right to be angry at all the injustices she had to endure, and she has the right to take positive steps to stop the abuse. Often it is when a woman recognizes that she is abused and that her husband's abuse is intentional that her anger motivates her to take control of her finances, file a restraining order, or develop a plan to leave.

As she moves forward, the abused woman must acknowledge her anger. She has to learn to express her anger in a safe environment and re-channel that anger in more productive ways. As she learns to deal with her anger effectively, she will be able to establish more appropriate boundaries and demand accountability for her mistreatment.

Lesson 6

Ephesian 4:26 (NLT) states, "Therefore each of you must put off falsehood and speak truthfully to his neighbor, for we are members of one body." The abused woman should speak the truth even if it creates conflict. She should speak her truth about the loss of her human dignity and self-respect and all the injustices she had to endure in her relationship. She must speak truthfully about her own experience, even if others do not understand or agree. She should not be afraid to confront those whose actions have triggered her anger.

Jesus disagreed with others on many occasions. In Matthew 15:1–11, Jesus spoke the truth. He was not afraid of offending people, including the powerful religious leaders of his own faith, the Pharisees. The disciples came to Jesus and asked, "Do you know that the Pharisees were offended when they heard this?" (In Matthew 15:12, NIV). Jesus replied, "Every plant that my father planted will be pulled up by the roots. Leave them: they are blind guides. If a blind man leads a blind man, both will fall in a pit" (verse 13). These passages from Ephesians and Matthew should help to strengthen the abused woman so that she is not afraid to challenge a behavior that violates human dignity and God's laws.

The abused woman may struggle with expressing her anger appropriately. For example, she might see the falsehood in her relationship at home and find it disconcerting to hear others remark about how great her partner is. Her challenge is to avoid slander without being deceptive. In her anger, she does not need to engage in purposeless slander of her husband. As Christian women, we are called to "rid yourselves of all such things as these: anger, rage, malice, slander, and filthy language from your lips" (Colossians 3:8, NIV). Also, we must remember: "In your anger do not sin" (Ephesians 4:26, NIV). Expressing anger should not lead to sinful actions like verbal abuse or fits of rage.

On the other hand, she should not mislead others by agreeing with their false perceptions of her husband or by denying her own feelings. She can state that something is false without going into detail about all her husband's failings. She also can state her feelings without losing her temper. She should consider her motive before speaking and should also consider the truthfulness of her comments. She is spiritually responsible for how she expresses her anger.

Steps for Handling Anger Within

The following steps are adapted from *Pattern Changing for Abused Women*.[7] I have elaborated on these steps and also used additional resources.

1. *Recognize the feeling of anger.* The abused woman must learn to recognize her anger and the way she was treated and give herself permission

to experience those angry feelings. She should not deny those feelings. A woman who has been in and out of touch with her anger may not be able to recognize anger about her own abuse, but she may be able to recognize anger for the mistreatment of her children and others.

Anger can be recognized by physical symptoms such as increased heart and respiration rate, increased blood pressure, muscle tension, and body temperature (which leads to perspiration and flushing), as well as by a sharpened, focused mind.[8] Recognizing the physical symptoms of anger can allow a woman to gain awareness that she is getting angry and to take steps to manage her anger before it takes control of her.

2. *Analyze the situation.* The woman must consider the reasons for her anger. What is she angry about? Whose problem is it? Does she have power over the situation or is she wasting her energy trying to control something she cannot control?

She cannot rid herself of anger until the cause is examined.[9] It is important that she carefully examine the reasons behind her anger and accept them. She may need professional help from a Christian or secular counselor to examine the root causes of ongoing anger issues.

3. *Release some of the internal anger energy.* As a Christian woman, she must find ways to release her anger regularly so that an explosion may be avoided. The Bible states: "Do not let the sun go down while you are still angry, and do not give the devil a foothold" (Ephesians 4:26-27, NIV). These scriptures are a reminder that suppressing and holding onto anger has spiritual consequences. The devil will use suppressed emotions to lead the abused Christian woman into sin and to harm her relationship with God.

As a Christian, she can release some anger by talking to other spiritual people. She can express her anger in a healthy way by using "I" statements. The "I" statements convey what she thinks and feels and that she is speaking for herself. These types of statements do not blame, accuse, or analyze the other person. For example, instead of stating "you always try to..." say "I feel really hurt when you say...."

She also can use scriptures and prayers to God to release her pain and to help her calm down and take control of her anger. She may find the book of Psalms helpful. The writers of this book demonstrate how to bring one's pain, shame, disappointment, rage, and sense of injury to God and ultimately attain peace and trust in God. Like the writers of Psalms, the abused woman needs opportunities to cry out to God and express her feelings.

Other ways to regularly release anger include exercising, screaming (alone), keeping a journal, thinking on things that are good, or doing something that helps her relax. The goal of these activities is to get rid of the immediate anger. The abused Christian woman must keep in mind, however, that taking action to address the cause of the anger is a critical first step and cannot be replaced by temporary actions to help her relax or forget her problems.

4. *Maintain a strong support network.* The abused woman must surround herself with supportive people and avoid non-supportive people while she is working to heal from her abuse and the resulting anger. Again, persistent or uncontrollable anger should be dealt with through counseling or therapy.

5. *Have a specific plan for dealing with anger-inducing situations before they occur.* The abused Christian woman must examine the situations that she did not handle well, learn from her mistakes, and develop a plan for handling a similar situation better next time. To develop the plan, she should consider, "What could I have done differently to keep from losing control and saying and doing things that I know are wrong and harmful?" She must learn to recognize when a situation is becoming too heated and when she needs to remove herself from the situation.[10]

She should *not* waste time considering "What could I have done differently so that the other person would behave differently?" She only can control her own anger and behavior, *not* someone else's. If she develops a specific plan but has difficulty following it, or cannot seem to develop a plan, she will need to explore the underlying factors that keep her from acting.

6. *Study and obey scriptures about anger:* James 1:19–21 (NIV) states, "My dear brothers, take note of this: Everyone should be quick to listen, slow to speak and to become angry, for a man's anger does not bring about the righteous life that God desires. Therefore, get rid of all moral filth and evil that is so prevalent and humbly accept the word planted in you, which can save you." The Word of God planted in the Christian woman has the ability to save her. Therefore, obedience to the scriptures has the power to help her let go of anger, find forgiveness for her abuser, and forgive herself.

Self-Reflection
1. What makes you angry? Make a list.
2. What is the real cause of your anger in these situations? Write down what you think. If you have trouble identifying the causes of your anger, consider the root of most human anger. Recall that anger is a normal response to the threat of physical and psychological harm. Unmet psychological needs for dignity, respect, and justice also can lead to anger. As an abused woman, all of those factors can be applied to your situation.
3. List the reasons for your anger in your abusive relationship. Did you express them? What was your spouse's response? Was it helpful?
4. How did you to cope with your anger in your abusive relationship? Did you suppress or deny it? List the physical and psychological symptoms you have experienced that may have been a result of denying or suppressing your anger.
5. Read Matthew 15:1–12 and write down your thoughts. During conflicts or disagreements do you speak the truth or are you afraid to speak the truth? The truth has to be told, even if your abuser does not listen or others do not believe your story.
6. Write your thoughts about Matthew 15:13. Jesus states, "If a blind man leads a blind man, both will fall into a pit." How have you allowed yourself to be controlled by your abuser's actions and words? Remember that allowing yourself to be negatively influenced by another's behavior will result in your downfall, as well as his.
7. How do you express anger? Do you wait until it is unbearable and then explode? Ephesians 4: 26 states, "In your anger do not sin."

8. Do you allow your anger to motivate you to seek change? What positive actions have you taken that were motivated by your anger?
9. Do you have a plan to manage the anger within yourself? What actions help you to effectively deal with your anger? If you have no plan, follow the suggestions in the text and evaluate how well they work for you. It is important to remember that if you have persistent or uncontrollable anger, you should seek professional help.
10. Read Colossians 3:8 and James 1:19–21 again and write down your thoughts. As a Christian woman, you have to develop convictions about anger and see anger from God's perspective. Use your convictions to help you re-channel your anger. Pray for courage and help as you seek this path. Also, ask others to pray for you.

Getting Rid of Anger: Scriptures for Encouragement

"To the Jews who had believed him, Jesus said, 'If you hold on to my teaching, you are really my disciples. Then you will know the truth and the truth will set you free'" (John 8:31–32, NIV). Speaking the truth is obeying Jesus' teachings, and he states that it will set you free. Search for your truth about your abuse. When you find it, you shouldn't be afraid to speak it out loud for everyone to hear. When you do this, you set yourself free from the chains that kept you in bondage.

"So stop telling lies. Let us tell our neighbors the truth, for we are all parts of the same body. And 'don't sin by letting anger control you.' Don't let the sun go down while you are still angry, for anger gives a foothold to the devil" (Ephesians 4:25–27, NLT). This is God's way of protecting you from the physical and psychological effects of anger, which may be caused by suppressing or denying it.

"Get rid of all bitterness, rage, anger, harsh words, and slander, as well as all types of evil behavior" (Ephesians 4:31, NLT). These behaviors keep you in emotional bondage; therefore, get rid of them!

"Arise, shine, for your light has come, and the glory of the Lord rises upon you. See, darkness covers the earth and thick darkness is over the peoples, but the Lord rises upon you and his glory appears over you" (Isaiah 60:1–2, NIV). Do not be ashamed to speak the truth about your abusive home, because the Lord has chosen you to stand up and his glory will let you shine. Don't let your anger stop you from reflecting His glory.

"Where is another God like you, who pardons the guilt of the remnant, overlooking the sins of his special people? You will not stay angry with your people forever, because you delight in showing unfailing love" (Micah 7:18, NLT). Just as God doesn't stay angry forever but delights in showing mercy and unfailing love, he does not want you to stay angry forever. He wants you to use his grace and love to set yourself free from your anger.

"The Lord is gracious and compassionate, slow to anger and rich in love. The Lord is good to all; he has compassion on all he has made" (Psalm 145:8–9, NIV). Extend the grace and love God has given you to others. In doing so, you will be equipped to deal with your anger and have the ability to forgive others.

"And now, dear brothers and sisters, one final thing. Fix your thoughts on what is true, and honorable, and right, and pure, and lovely, and admirable. Think about things that are excellent and worthy of praise. Keep putting into practice all you learned and received from me—everything you heard from me and saw me doing. Then the God of peace will be with you" (Philippians 4:8–9, NIV). A key to attack angry thoughts is to change your thinking. Think of God's blessings and the positive steps you are taking to change and heal and pray for God's peace as you move on.

Forgiveness Is a Process

Lesson 7

A Christian woman is asked to repent in many ways, including forgiving those who wronged her and seeking forgiveness from those she has wronged. She is to forgive because God has forgiven her. It is never right and it is unchristian to withhold forgiveness. The abused Christian woman, however, might say she has forgiven her abuser but finds herself continuing to experience the painful emotions linked to the hurt(s) she has experienced. When she thinks about her abuse, why does she still feel pain, anger, sadness, guilt, or a sense of shame? Why does she have more difficulty with forgiveness than others who have not experienced domestic violence? The abused Christian woman may have difficulty because she was not taught to view forgiveness as a process and needs to understand that to experience true forgiveness, her emotional healing is essential.

To understand this process, we will examine premature forgiveness and Jesus' teachings about forgiveness. Some of the materials in this section are adapted from *No Place for Abuse* by Catherine Clark Kroeger and Nancy Nason-Clark and from Pamela Cooper-White's *Women Healing and Empowering*. As we examine the forgiveness process, we will look at the story of Jacob and Esau in the book of Genesis.

Premature Forgiveness

Premature forgiveness is linked to our denial mechanisms,[11] which are part of our defense mechanisms. Defense mechanisms are psychological techniques we use, both consciously and unconsciously, to protect us from thoughts or feelings we are unable to tolerate.[12]

Denial is common among victims of abuse. For example, after a woman is badly beaten, her husband might say he is sorry and will never do it again. The abused woman may say she forgives him, and she may push the thoughts and feelings related to the beating out of her mind. She tells herself she has forgiven him, perhaps out of a desire to make things OK, avoid conflict, and/or to avoid dealing with the emotional effects of the assault.

This premature forgiveness is itself a form of denial.[13] Denial is refusing to accept the reality that painful thoughts and feelings do exist. Denial says her experience did not happen.[14] The abused woman may be stuck in denial when she does not work through the process of forgiveness.

Adding to the abused Christian woman's human tendency to avoid psychological pain, an incomplete understanding of some scriptures might also lead her to forgive prematurely. For example, in Matthew 18:21–22, Jesus tells us to forgive seventy times seven. This scripture on forgiveness can be taken out of context to convince the abused woman that she simply needs to "forgive and forget."[15] Other Christians attempting to help or counsel the woman may be uncomfortable with the abused woman's extreme anger and fear and may be caught up in denial themselves.

If we look more closely at his teachings, we see that Jesus placed forgiveness in the context of a larger process for justice and healing.[16] He described a specific process for dealing with someone who has wronged someone else:

> If another believer sins against you, go privately and point out the offense. If the other person listens and confesses it, you have won that person back. But if you are unsuccessful, take one or two others with you and go back again, so that everything you say may be confirmed by two or three witnesses. If the person still refuses to listen, take your case to the church. Then if he or she won't accept the church's decision, treat that person as a pagan or a corrupt tax collector. (Matthew 18:15–17, NLT)

The process Jesus describes involves first stating the hurt to the person who wronged you. If the person listens, acknowledges the hurt, asks for forgiveness, and repents, you must forgive him. If your efforts are not effective, Jesus teaches to take two or three witnesses and state your hurt again. If the person still refuses to listen, you are to take the issue to the church. If the church decides that you are right (i.e., the person has indeed wronged you) and he still refuses to listen, acknowledge his sin, and repent, then you are to have nothing to do with that person. At the end of this process, if that person *cannot or will not change*, you are under no obligation to continue to have a relationship with him. In the case of domestic abuse, if the abuser refuses to repent, the abused

Christian woman has moral rights and an obligation to seek help. If the abuser does not repent, she can pursue a legal separation.

The abused woman may be stuck at the beginning of the forgiveness process regarding her abuse. Although the scriptures cited earlier provide a process for forgiving, she needs to understand that this process is not always possible. The person who hurt her may not be open to participating in the process or is no longer around. In some cases, following this process might not be safe. The abused woman may never have the opportunity to express her hurt to the abuser.

On the other hand, the abused woman cannot cut every unrepentant person out of her life for minor infractions and annoying habits, especially if they are not Christians. For example, she does not abandon minor children if they do not repent of disobedience. She does not stop calling her mother because she will not apologize for or admit her parenting mistakes. She does not divorce her husband simply because he fails to acknowledge and repent of every careless word he ever spoke to her.

Forgiveness is not something the woman can achieve by her own effort, but she needs forgiveness to start her healing process. Healing will require a lot of work and planning. It is important for the abused woman to pray to God and ask the Holy Spirit to guide her as she starts the healing process. She also needs to seek help from others: "Confess your sins to each other, and pray for each other so you may be healed" (James 5:16, NLT).

Forgiveness: The Example of Jacob and Esau

As we examine the forgiveness process, we will look at the story of Jacob and Esau found in Genesis. This story portrays the process of true forgiveness. In Genesis 25:27–33, Esau sells his birthright. Genesis 25:29 (NLT) states that "Esau arrived home exhausted and hungry from a hunt." Because of his desire for food, he was not thinking clearly. Jacob knew his brother Esau's state of mind and body, and he took advantage of Esau, using his brother's physical need to manipulate him into selling him his birthright in exchange for food. In Genesis 27:1–29, Jacob steals Esau's blessings with the help of his mother, who manipulates their father, her husband.

Doing the Work: Anger, Forgiveness, and Grieving

Like Esau, a woman may feel that others manipulated her into making foolish choices. She may realize that family and friends manipulated her into doing something when she was young and easily influenced, which she later has come to regret. Her need for love may have led her to be manipulated in a relationship. Physical, psychological, or sexual abuse also leads to a loss of identity and self-worth, which makes a woman more vulnerable to manipulation. Regardless of the reasons for her bad choices, the woman will need to forgive herself and others and begin the healing process.

The Process

"The first step toward forgiveness is simply acknowledging to yourself that you have been hurt."[17] Esau became angry when he realized what his brother had done. Esau said, "Isn't he rightly named Jacob? He has deceived me two times: He took my birthright, and now he's taken my blessing!" (Genesis 27:36, NIV). The abused woman has the right to acknowledge that she has been wronged and to express her anger toward those who have hurt her. Although the Bible does not say what a man named Alexander did to Paul, Paul is willing to acknowledge his hurt and who harmed him. He acknowledges that, "Alexander the coppersmith did me much harm" (2 Timothy 4:14a, NLT). The abused woman will need to state to others her hurts, pain, and the physical and emotional effects of her abuse by her husband.

If the abused woman experiences difficulty identifying the hurt and the people involved, she might need to carefully evaluate the emotions that continue to surface. For example, she should consider certain events or behaviors that cause her to react in a way that is out of proportion to the importance of that event or behavior. Disproportionate reactions to real or imagined wrongs often are signals that a woman is responding to a deep emotional hurt.[18] Once she identifies the hurt linked to her over-reaction, she can begin the process of forgiveness.

The abused woman needs to clearly understand her role and the roles of others in the action that caused her pain, if she is to acknowledge her own mistakes and repent. Esau did not show concern for his own actions. He did not take responsibility for the consequences of selling his birthright. Perhaps if he had, the story would have turned out differently: "Jacob gave Esau some bread and lentil stew. Esau ate the meal, then got up and left. He showed contempt for his rights as the firstborn" (Genesis 25:34, NLT).

The woman also must understand *what is not her fault or responsibility*. She cannot blame herself for the actions of those who have wronged her. Unmerited self-blame is evident in relationships where there is psychological, physical, and/or sexual abuse. The abused woman may say, "If I had been more loving, kind, or forgiving, he wouldn't have said those hurtful words to me." However, as discussed earlier in this book, the abuser speaks abusively, regardless of her behavior, because of his own anger and desire for control.

It may be difficult to clearly identify and accept each party's responsibility in a painful event. The abused woman, however, must try. She must recognize that, in most cases, she is responsible for allowing her emotional reactions to her abuse to control her life. For example, the emotional effects of the abuse may still have a hold on the woman's life long after she has left the relationship. She is not responsible for the abuse itself because she did not have the power to stop her abuser. But, as a Christian, she will have to take the responsibility for repairing the emotional damage resulting from the abuse and allowing God to heal her. She repents by trusting God and asking him to free her from the emotional impact of the abuse.

If the abused woman is confused about her responsibilities, she may continue to hold on to vengeful feelings. Do not seek revenge! God will take care of that person. Paul ends his complaint about the person who wronged him by stating his conviction that the "Lord will pay him back for his deeds" (2 Timothy 4:14b, NLT). In a number of passages, the Bible discourages the Christian from getting even. For example, Leviticus 19:18 (NLT) states, "Never seek revenge or bear a grudge against anyone, but love your neighbor as yourself. I am the Lord." While Deuteronomy 32:35 (NLT) counsels, "I will take vengeance; I will repay those who deserve it. In due time their feet will slip. Their day of disaster will arrive, and their destiny will overtake them."

The abused woman may experience a real struggle of faith with regard to vengeance. Even though she may struggle, she *must* safely leave this matter to God's hands. Examining the story, we find Esau struggling with revenge: "From that time on, Esau hated Jacob because their father had given Jacob the blessing. And Esau began to scheme: 'I will soon be mourning my father's death. Then I will kill my brother, Jacob'" (Genesis 27:41, NLT). His mother intervened by helping Jacob to flee. Esau apparently let go of his vengeful feelings, because he did not go after his brother when Jacob left home.

In Genesis 32, we see Jacob struggling with the consequence of his sins. In verse 11 he says, "O Lord, please rescue me from the hand of my brother, Esau. I am afraid that he is coming to attack me, along with my wives and children" (NLT). Jacob had all the blessings, yet when he had to go back home, he still struggled with fear. It was on his way back home that he wrestled with God (Genesis 32:22–31). God dealt with Jacob so that he ultimately was forced to return home, face his brother, and ask him for forgiveness. The abused woman must find comfort knowing that her abuser will have to engage in his own struggle with God. He ultimately may choose to repent, or he may not.

The ability to forgive is an act of faith. If the woman is struggling with her faith, she will have to strengthen her faith before completing the forgiveness process. Understanding God's grace also is essential. "The ability to forgive comes from God in a *long-term* work of grace."[19] God's purpose for Christians is to receive his grace and to extend that grace to others.

When Isaac blesses Esau, he predicts that Esau ". . . will live by the sword. You will serve your brother for a time, but then you will shake loose from him and be free" (Genesis 27:40, NLT). How was Esau set free? It was the work of God and the result of Isaac's blessings. God has blessed the abused woman with forgiveness as the result of his son's death on the cross. The abused Christian woman must strive to understand the importance of God's blessing of forgiveness because it has the power to help her forgive. The blessing of forgiveness is free, but she will have to make the choice to receive that forgiveness.

The abused Christian woman will need to experience God's work of grace on a timetable that is not hers to determine. Others may have difficulty understanding this fact. It was twenty years before Esau met Jacob again. Jacob did not ask Esau for forgiveness before leaving home. Esau had to work though his own process of forgiveness before Jacob's return.

Ultimately, if she is to heal, the abused woman must choose to let go of the damage, anger, resentment, helplessness, bitterness, hopelessness, guilt, and shame that have resulted from her abuse and affected her life. When she chooses to let go, she will be free to receive God's blessings of peace, joy, happiness, and self-fulfillment.

In Genesis 33:10 (NLT), "Jacob insisted, 'No, if I have found favor with you, please accept this gift from me. And what a relief to see your friendly smile. It is like seeing the face of God!'" Jacob knew when he saw his brother's face that his brother had forgiven him. "To 'forgive' means to put something away, set it free, as well as to put one thing aside in order to move on to something else."[20] As for the abused woman, forgiveness essentially means putting away her anger, fears, and doubts that bind her to her abuser and to others who have hurt her, so that those things no longer control her life.[21] Esau chose to let go and to free himself from his brother's grip. By doing this he was able to move forward and receive his blessings. Only by forgiving in this way can the abused woman move on to something better.

Remember that breaking free can be a long and difficult process. But, with prayer and support from others, the abused woman can break free! As she goes through this process, she may find that she is taking baby steps like a child who is learning to walk. The child falls constantly, but the parent is there to encourage the child to get up and try again. God will be that encouraging parent for her.

Self-Reflection

This section covers the general forgiveness process, which will include forgiving the experiences of spousal abuse as well as other experiences in life where the woman might need to forgive and seek healing. A woman might struggle for a long period of time to forgive specific behaviors of the abusive husband, not because of the seriousness of the act, but because these behaviors relate to hurts she experienced in the past. This "self-reflection" will require more thought and consideration of past hurts. This process may be very difficult for abused women who have experienced severe trauma prior to the abusive relationship. In these cases, the woman may want to work through this section with a licensed therapist. In addition, if the woman has been diagnosed with or suspects she might be suffering from a mental illness such as major depression, she should seek professional help.

1. When you think about those who have hurt you, do you still feel the emotions associated with the incident? What types of emotions resurface? Write down the incidents, those involved, the feelings you recall experiencing at the time of the event, and your reactions. Be careful to separate facts from emotions.

2. Look at what you wrote for question one. Consider what you read earlier in this section about denial. If recalling the event produces no emotions in you or produces numbness, you are in denial. Or, if you recall an intense incident where you or someone else was physically hurt or experienced an intense episode of name-calling, threats, and intimidation, and you make excuses for this behavior, you are in denial.

3. Write down your thoughts about Matthew 18:15–18. These scriptures were addressed to Christians but can be applied to non-Christians as well. Are these scriptures possible or impossible to follow? Do you think this kind of teaching could be applied to a marital relationship?

4. Read Genesis 27:36 and 2 Timothy 4:14a again. The process Jesus describes begins with stating your hurt to the person who wronged you. Are you stuck in the beginning of this process? Look at what you wrote for the first question. Did you name people who have hurt you and to whom you never had the opportunity to express your feelings? What has kept you from confronting them? Or, if you did confront them, how did they respond? Was it helpful to you or not? What about your abuse? Did you confront your husband or ex-husband and honestly share your feelings and how the abuse affected you? If not, why? If you did, what was his response? You might have legitimate reasons for not confronting your abuser, such as fear of psychological or physical abuse. Recall that going through the formal process of confronting someone

who sinned against you, as described in the Bible, is not always possible or wise.

5. Consider the incidents you described in question one. You may benefit by expressing the hurt you experienced to someone other than the abuser. Find a safe place and person to whom you can express your feelings—someone you can trust. You might benefit from expressing your feelings through journaling and then sharing the journal with another trusted person. It is important, however, to get other people involved in your healing process. Trusted friends, mentors, and sisters in Christ can provide great support and guidance. An abused woman, however, must recognize that only other women who have walked in her shoes can fully empathize with and validate her experiences. The abused woman may find this kind of support at a domestic violence center or a Christian-based group for abused women. When talking to others, be honest about your feelings. Acknowledge the effects of the hurt on your emotional and spiritual wellbeing.

6. (Back to the first question again!) Look at the events and your emotional reactions to those events. Be careful to avoid focusing on your emotional representations of the events. When you are overly emotional, it is difficult to see your responsibility. Write down what you are responsible for and what is not your responsibility. Focus on your responsibilities because that is where your power lies. Responsibility should not be linked to guilt but to recognition of your own power to change.

7. Search for the need behind the emotion and the specific hurt. For example, behind anger there is a deeper need for significance and value that is violated when a woman is belittled or ignored. Behind a feeling of sadness may be need for love or hope, which is violated when a woman is continually rejected or disappointed by her husband or others she cares about. God has the power to meet those needs. Write down the need behind the hurts you described in question one.

8. Examine the root of emotions that are especially intense or persistent. If you are struggling to forgive, dig deeper for the root of your difficulty. Finding the root is important because that is place where the healing will occur. The root of some emotions may lie in unresolved events in early life. For example, as a child a woman may have been told, "You are so stupid that you will never achieve anything good." That kind of statement has a significant negative impact on her self-worth and may lead to strong reactions when she feels "stupid" as an adult. As another example, a woman who was ignored or neglected by family members as a child may be more hurt by her abuser's ignoring her than by a physical attack. Or, a woman who was raped may be especially devastated when her abuser calls her a "whore."

   To complete her healing, the abused woman also must forgive the people involved in those painful early life events. Examine what you wrote in response to the first question. What events that occurred prior to your abusive relationship might be triggers for intense reactions or stumbling blocks to forgiving certain types of hurts?

9. Acknowledge any spiritual struggle with God. This may involve expressing anger or a lack of trust toward God for allowing bad things to happen to you.

10. Read 2 Timothy 4:14b, Leviticus 19:18, Deuteronomy 32:35, and Genesis 27:41. When you reflect on the people who have hurt you, do you have thoughts of revenge? What have you done about those thoughts? Remember that revenge is not your role; it is God's.

    Read Genesis 32:22–31. Bring your thoughts and plans to God. Find comfort in knowing that the person who hurt you will have to face the consequences of his sins. Release that person to God. God will deal with him in his own way and timing.

11. Read Genesis 27:40. Are you aware that you cannot achieve forgiveness on your own? Do you believe that the cross is a "free gift" that enables you to forgive? Reflect on the sufferings that Jesus had to endure to save you. He suffered physical pain, false

accusations, being spat on, name-calling, and hurtful jokes. Most abused women can relate to these sufferings. Choose to continually reflect on the cross as you work on forgiving the people you named. Remember that forgiving others is being obedient to God's commands, as stated in Colossians 3:2, "Make allowance for each other's faults, and forgive anyone who offends you. Remember, the Lord forgave you, so you must forgive others." Pray and ask others to pray for you as you embark on this challenge.

12. Read Genesis 33:10. Look at what you wrote about the needs behind your hurts. Bring those needs to God. Pray that he meets those needs. Replace any false beliefs about yourself with his truths found in the scriptures. For example, when the abused woman feels like she has no value, the scriptures say she does. Ephesians 2:10 says she is God's "masterpiece", and James 1:18 states she is his "prized possession." She has to hold on to God's truths to get rid of her feeling of insignificance.

13. Again, ask others to pray for you. Ask the Holy Spirit to help you to let go of all the emotions like ungodly anger, resentment, guilt, bitterness, and shame that bind you to the hurt, and to fill you with the fruits of the spirit as in Galatians 5:22, "… love, joy, peace, patience, kindness, faithfulness, gentleness and self-control." Remember the earlier definition of "forgiveness": "to put something away, set it free, as well as to put one thing aside in order to move on to something else."[22] Set your damaged emotions free!

I pray, as you work through this process, that God surrounds you with grace and peace and grants you the release of all the emotions that bind you to your abuser and to those who have hurt you. I pray that you experience the process of forgiveness and remember that there is no timetable except God's.

Forgiveness, Setting Yourself Free: Scriptures for Encouragement

"Therefore, since we have a great high priest who has gone through the heavens, Jesus the Son of God, let us hold firmly to the faith we profess. For we do not have a high priest who is unable to sympathize with our weaknesses, but we have one who has been tempted in every way, just as we are—yet was without sin. Let us then approach the throne of grace with confidence, so that we may receive mercy and find grace to help us in our time of need" (Hebrews 4:14–16, NIV). We have a high priest who understands and can relate to your weaknesses. He faced the same testing and emotions you have experienced. This fact should give you hope as you approach him for forgiveness and healing.

"Be kind and compassionate to one another, forgiving each other, just as in Christ God forgave you. Be imitators of God, therefore, as dearly loved children and live a life of love, just as Christ loved us and gave himself up for us as a fragrant offering and sacrifice to God" (Galatians 6:4, NIV). Use the cross to forgive others and yourself. Forgiving others is being obedient to God's commands.

"You were dead because of your sins and because your sinful nature was not yet cut away. Then God made you alive with Christ, for he forgav all our sins. He canceled the record of the charges against us and took it away by nailing it to the cross. In this way, he disarmed the spiritual rulers and authorities. He shamed them publicly by his victory over them on the cross" (Colossians 2:13–15, NLT). Your debt of sins committed was canceled by Christ's death on the cross and you were set free. Forgive yourself. Don't continue to hold on to the hurt, anger, and pain that binds you to your abusive relationship. Forgive and let go because Christ has forgiven you.

"You are a God, gracious and compassionate. Slow to anger and abounding in love" (Nehemiah 9:17, NIV). God is slow to anger. He has *limitless* patience, compassion and love. Use his attributes to forgive yourself and others.

"You are forgiving and good, O Lord, abounding in love to all who call to you" (Psalm 86:5, NIV). Both of the above passages show that God is forgiving, good, and abounding in love. When you have trouble forgiving, remember God's nature and let that encourage your heart to forgive.

"The Lord appeared to us in the past, saying: 'I have loved you with an everlasting love; I have drawn you with unfailing kindness'" (Jeremiah 31:3, NIV). Let God's love and kindness encourage you as you go through the process of forgiveness.

"... Do not forget the helpless. Why does the wicked man revile God? Why does he say to himself, 'He won't call me to account'? But you, O God, do see trouble and grief; you consider it to take it in hand. The victim commits himself to you; you are the helper of the fatherless. Break the arm of the wicked and evil man; call him to account for his wickedness that would not be found out" (Psalm 10:12–15, NIV). You may not understand why God allowed your abuser to get away with his abusive behaviors. It seems he has no accountability. But, God knows and sees your trouble and grief and he will help you. Commit yourself to him and forgive your abuser. Your abuser will have to pay the consequences for his sins on God's timetable, not yours.

Grieving: The Act of Letting Go

EDITH

I HAD DONE A LOT of healing work. I had forgiven my ex-husband and others who had played some role in earlier painful events that I had difficulty letting go of. My self-esteem was strengthened and my faith was strong. I had accepted the fact that I was an abused woman, educated myself about the effects of domestic violence, and sought help. I no longer felt ashamed to talk about my abuse. Regardless of all these changes, I felt something was missing. I didn't feel closure in my healing process.

Years later, I recognized that I didn't complete the grieving process. I was aware that grieving was needed for losses such as death of a loved one, or divorce, but I wasn't aware that grieving a "domestic violence" relationship was a necessary part of the healing process. Subconsciously I was actively grieving while in the relationship. For example, I had to deal with the realization that I was an abused woman. I also dealt with anger and sadness for all the suffering I had experienced. I had to let go of the dream of the white-picket-fence-family and the desire to find meaning in my experience of the abuse.

A crisis event in my ex-husband's life revealed what was holding me back from completing the grieving process and moving on. In truth, I still was holding on to the dream that he could play the nurturing father role in the lives of the kids. I didn't want to grieve and let go of the idea of a father who has empathy for his children's pain and difficulties, engages in their social and athletic activities, and guides them as they navigate their complex world.

As I look back, I wanted my ex-husband to be actively involved in the lives of the kids. I made a conscious effort to make sure that the visitation plan was implemented. On many occasions the kids were left with disappointments. Canceled visits, unreturned phone calls, missed birthdays, and non-participation in school activities was the norm in their relationship with their father. He rarely asked about how they were doing in school, discussed their feelings or life goals, or verbalized his share of the responsibility for the pain they were experiencing.

After the few visits with him, they came home filled with sadness instead of joy. As a result, it was difficult to see them go to visits because, when they returned, we all had to relive the painful emotions that the visits provoked.

As the kids grew older, the desire to visit their father dwindled. I still held on to the dream that he could change and be a good father to them. It was painful to recognize that this would never happen. The reality was I was expecting my ex-husband to be a father when he did not know how to be one. He did not practice the skills needed to become a good father. As a result, there was a huge dent in his relationship with his children that would take a lot of hard work to mend. The responsibility of developing a relationship and sustaining that relationship with the kids was his. I could only be there to provide emotional support, help them verbalize their pain and disappointments, and make appropriate referrals to help them work on their own healing process.

When I let go of the dream of a good father for my children, I felt free to move on and find closure. I am aware that the psychological effects of the children's relationship with their father are enormous. I pray that at some point in their lives they will see God as their father, a father who understands their pain and will always be there for them and love them more than their earthly father and I ever can.

The Importance of Grieving and Mourning

Grief is a normal reaction to any kind of loss. Grief is caused by conflicting emotions at the end of a change, as with the loss of a loved one or through divorce.[23] "Grieving allows the woman to 'clear the decks' both internally and externally. Internally it helps her move to a greater peace of mind. Externally, for the abused woman, it helps pave the way for steps toward safety and fuller living."[24]

Both mourning and grieving are needed to express and experience the emotions of our loss. Grief is a woman's personal experience with loss. Mourning is the public expression of grief.[25] Western culture places emphasis on self-sufficiency and independence. Individuals often are made to feel weak or ashamed when they express their sadness or when they express that they are frightened or need help. They are encouraged to "snap out of it." No one can really "snap out of" anything. They usually bury their feelings, which may resurface as a chronic physical or mental illness or as acute emotional distress.[26] Unresolved grief festers like a deep wound covered by scar tissue that occasionally breaks open as the hidden emotions are discharged.[27] When this happens, a woman may feel anxious, tense, fearful, angry, confused, sad, guilty, resentful, or empty.[28]

Grieving over an abusive relationship may be especially difficult because this type of grief generally is not accepted in Western society. The sense of shame and failure that often results from an abusive relationship also may prevent a woman from fully mourning and grieving the losses associated with that relationship. To complicate her dilemma, she may believe that it is wrong to grieve her abuse, which prevents her from completing the grieving process.[28]

The Bible encourages mourning and grieving: "Blessed are those who mourn, for they will be comforted" (Matthew 5:4, NIV). Jesus calls to us to "Come to me, all you who are weary and burdened, and I will give you rest" (Matthew 11:28, NIV). Psalm 34:18 (NIV) states, "The Lord is close to the brokenhearted and saves those who are crushed in spirit." God demonstrates his comfort when a Christian woman is mourning and grieving. Grieving work, however, requires courage and strength. Jesus will help the woman as she walks through this process.

He is willing to heal the woman from the pain of her loss: "Though you have made me see troubles many and bitter, you will restore my life again; from the depths of the earth you will again bring me up. You will increase my honor and comfort me once more" (Psalm 71:20-21, NIV). God will comfort the woman and give her honor, regardless of her losses.

At the end of the grieving process there is joy: "All you saints! Sing your hearts out to God! Thank him to his face! He gets angry once in a while, but across a lifetime there is only love. The nights of crying your eyes out give way to days of laughter" (Psalm 30:5, *The Message*). Jeremiah 31:13 (NIV) promises, "Then young women will dance and be glad, young men and old as well. I will turn their mourning into gladness; I will give them comfort and joy instead of sorrow."

When she is done with her grieving process, she can use the same comfort God gave her to help others who are experiencing the pain of a loss: "Praise be to the God and Father of our Lord Jesus Christ, the Father of compassion and the God of all comfort, who comforts us in all our troubles, so that we can comfort those in any trouble with the comfort we ourselves receive from God" (2 Corinthians 1:3-4, NIV).

Lesson 8

To start the grieving process, the woman must identify her losses. Some women may have difficulty identifying their losses and may need professional help. For the abused woman, identifying the loss is difficult when the individual responsible for the loss is still around inflicting physical or psychological abuse. She may be so preoccupied with dealing with his abusive behavior that she does not recognize her own grief and related emotions. The process of grieving is a conscious effort. Self-reflection is necessary for the woman to identify her losses. In fact, it may take her years to become aware of them.

For the woman, "grief over an abusive relationship involves, not only remembering and fully acknowledging her hurts, but also grieving the dreams that have been broken by the abuse. It means being real about her hopes and mourning the loss of what she may have given up to change."[30] She has to grieve about the dreams she had for her relationship, dreams that have been broken by the abuse. For example, the woman may grieve about the loss of trust and the hope for a loving relationship.[31] She may need to grieve for the loss of her identity and self-respect as a result of the abuse. The woman also will need to mourn and grieve for herself because of the pain she had to endure. Finally, she may need to grieve what she has lost because of the abusive relationship (e.g., opportunities for work, travel, her youth, future financial security, etc.).

If she has left the relationship, she may need to grieve the loss of a lover and a companion. She will have to grieve the loss of dreams of a partner who is present "in sickness and health," and who leads the family. She will have to grieve the loss of some of the dreams she had for her children (i.e., growing up in a nurturing, two-parent family). The ideal of a father who is emotionally and physically present to help her children as they navigate life may never come to pass. She also may need to grieve the loss of some possessions and, in some cases, the financial security her partner provided.

The Grief Recovery Handbook states, "There are no absolutes in grief. There are no reactions so universal that all, or even most, will experience them."[32] There also is no set timeframe for grieving. The abused woman needs time to grieve her losses. Each woman may begin and complete her grieving process at different points. She might have started the grieving process long before she left the relationship. Next she may need to complete the process by consciously expressing, remembering, and performing a symbolic (ritual) representation of her losses in order to let go and move on.

The stages of grief outlined below present some feelings and thoughts that the woman may experience as she goes through the grieving process. There is no specific order for this process and not everyone will experience all the stages exactly as they are described.

Stages of Grief

The following stages have been adapted from *Healing the Child Within* by Charles L. Whitfield. I have attempted to apply these stages to the abused woman's situation in the detailed descriptions following each stage.[33]

Stage 1: shock, alarm, and denial. The woman recognizes that something is wrong with her relationship. She begins to accept that she is a victim of domestic violence. The woman becomes increasingly aware of the abuse in her relationship and its psychological and physical effects on her and her children. She recognizes that the hopes and dreams she had for the relationship may never be realized.

Stage 2: acute grief. Grief involves physical and psychological pain and distress. At this stage, the abused woman may experience restlessness, anxiety and depression, and an inability to concentrate. She may cry often, become unusually fearful or angry, and feel extreme guilt and shame. The woman searches to make sense of what is happening and may have a compulsion to find meaning in what she has endured. She also may desire a "miracle" to change her situation, blame herself for the failed relationship, and feel lost, helpless, hopeless, and confused.

Stage 3: integration of the loss and grief. Integration occurs when the woman accepts the reality of the loss and moves on to living a functional and positive life. Not all of the emotions associated with grieving will disappear, but their intensity will diminish. Actual evidence of change or transformation is seen in this stage; for example, the ability to enjoy life, to grow from the experience, and to take care of physical and emotional needs.

For the abused woman, transformation will involve changing her perceptions of how she sees herself and her abuse. She will be able to tell her story without shame or humiliation and to forgive her abuser and herself. The woman will realize that she is no longer controlled by fear but will acknowledge it and release her fears to God and other friends and family that she feels safe with. She will develop a clearer understanding of her true strengths and weaknesses. The woman will learn to honestly express her emotions and let go of what she cannot control. She will begin to recognize when she needs to seek physical, psychological, and financial help for herself and her children.

As she develops a belief in her capabilities, she becomes empowered to make the right choices. One obvious example of making better choices will be an increased interest in caring for her body and spirit by being physically active, eating healthy, engaging in social activities, learning new skills, and developing new, positive interests. The Christian woman will also take care of her spiritual needs by using scriptures to attack negative self-talk. At the end of the process, the most important accomplishment for the woman will be knowing and accepting that she no longer is an abused woman or a victim but a conqueror of domestic abuse.

As she works through the stages of grief, it is important that the woman acknowledge her emotions without judging them or trying to push them away. As a Christian woman, it is equally important that she express her emotions to others and God. In addition to verbally sharing her feelings with others and with God in prayer, she can write, journal, draw, or engage in other activities that allow her to express and release her emotions.

In the scriptures there are many examples of individuals who mourned and grieved and were not afraid to express their emotions. They wanted others to be aware, through their appearance and actions that they were mourning and grieving. For example:

> Job got up and tore his robe and shaved his head. Then he fell to the ground in worship and said: "Naked I came from my mother's womb, and naked I will depart. The Lord gave and the Lord has taken away; may the name of the Lord be praised." (Job 1:20–21, NIV)

> When they saw him from a distance, they could hardly recognize him; they began to weep aloud, and they tore their robes and sprinkled dust on their heads. Then they sat on the ground with him for seven days and seven nights. No one said a word to him, because they saw how great his suffering was. (Job 2:12–13, NIV)

> Jacob tore his clothes, put on sackcloth and mourned for his son many days. All his sons and daughters came to comfort him, but he refused to be comforted. "No," he said, "I will continue to mourn until I join my son in the grave." So his father wept for him. (Genesis 37:34–35, NIV)

(Putting on sackcloth was a symbolic representation that a person was mourning and grieving.)

The abused Christian woman also should express her grief in ways that are meaningful to her and allow others see her suffering so they can offer comfort. As she works through the transformation stage, the woman can choose to perform a ritual that symbolizes her healing. That ritual could be planting a tree to represent her new life, creating a mourning ritual with friends, or burning or burying the list of all the painful memories that she has released. She also should reward herself for the hard work of healing by engaging in activities that bring her joy. Once grieving is done, her eyes will open to envision a better future for herself and her children.

Self-Reflection

1. Were you aware that mourning and grieving your abusive relationship is necessary to complete the healing process?
2. Were you shocked when you first realized that you were a victim of domestic abuse? What types of emotions did you experience after discovering this fact?
3. Can you recall the dreams you had when you entered the relationship, dreams that have been broken by the abuse? Make a list of those lost dreams. Be real about the hopes and dreams you had that never came to pass for the relationship. Fully acknowledge the emotions associated with your loss, such as pain, sadness, confusion, helplessness, and disappointment. Give yourself permission to experience those emotions. Which emotional wounds do you want healed? Acknowledge the pain you had to endure and mourn the hopes and dreams you abandoned.

   - In the book, *Women Healing and Empowering: Domestic Violence: Participant Guide*, the author, Pamela Cooper-White, outlines the process of dealing with and letting go of painful memories:[34] *Express the memory (e.g., journaling, sharing).* Find effective ways to express the emotions associated with the memory. For the Christian woman, expressing the emotions associated with the memory to others and to God is important.

- Perform an act of healing that is visual or tactile. (e.g., plant a tree.)
- Celebrate. (e.g., have a party, do something positive that you enjoy.)

4. The end stage of mourning and grieving is transformation or change. It is very important for your physical and mental health that you make this transformation. Letting go of unrealistic dreams and creating new dreams is necessary for change. Think ahead five years.[35]

- What are your new dreams?
- What would you like your life to be like?
- Who would you have in your life?
- Where would you spend significant time?
- What would you need to change in order to make this happen?
- What might have to be lost or given up?

When the grieving and mourning process is completed, as previously stated, you are no longer an abused woman or a victim but a *conqueror* of domestic abuse. Live your life as a free woman in Christ!

Moving On: Scriptures for Encouragement

"As a deer pants for streams of water, so my soul pants for you, O God. My soul thirsts for God, for the living God. Where can I go and meet with God?" (Psalm 42:1-2, NIV). Thirst for God as you grieve. He is right beside you to comfort your spirit and fill your emptiness.

"Praise the Lord, my soul; all my inmost being, praise his holy name. Praise the Lord, my soul, and forget not all his benefits—who forgives all your sins and heals all your diseases, who redeems your life from the pit and crowns you with love and compassion, who satisfies your desires with good things so that your youth is renewed like the eagle's. The Lord works righteousness and justice for all the oppressed" (Psalm 103:1-6, NIV). God forgives sins, heals all diseases, saves you from your darkest pit and crowns you with love and compassion, strengthens and renews you, provides the desires of your heart, and will seek justice on your behalf. That is the kind of God you serve!

"I, Jesus, have sent my angel to give you this testimony for the churches. I am the Root and the Offspring of David, and the bright Morning Star. The Spirit and the bride say, 'Come!' And let him who hears say, 'Come!' Whoever is thirsty, let him come; and whoever wishes, let him take the free gift of the water of life" (Revelation 22:16–17, NIV). Jesus is the root of our existence. He is our bright morning star. He will brighten every difficulty or pain we face. He fills our thirsty souls with the springs of living water. Our call is to come to him for this living water and get healing. Remain in Him and stay committed to Him and you will inherit all of this and more.

"In my distress I called to the Lord, and he answered me. From deep in the realm of the dead I called for help, and you listened to my cry" (Jonah 2:2, NIV). In your suffering and distress, God is willing to listen to you and help you.

"God is our refuge and strength, an ever-present help in trouble. Therefore we will not fear, though the earth give way and the mountains fall into the heart of the sea" (Psalm 46:1–2, NIV). God is your refuge and strength as you face healing. Though things around you appear to be crumbling, do not be afraid; he is there to bring you to safety and set you free.

"Peace I leave with you; my peace I give you. I do not give to you as the world gives. Do not let your hearts be troubled and do not be afraid" (John 14:27, NIV). Move on with your new life, knowing that Christ is with you. He will embrace you with his peace on this new path.

"Therefore, if anyone is in Christ, the new creation has come: The old has gone, the new is here!" (2 Corinthians 5:17, NIV). God has set you free. You no longer have to live your old life. Live your life as a free woman in Christ.

CHAPTER 8

HOW CAN THE COMMUNITY HELP THE ABUSED CHRISTIAN WOMAN?

In this chapter we will focus on the role of the community as the woman seeks assistance and healing. The "community" means those who are willing to help the Christian woman and includes family, friends, Christian brothers and sisters, hot-line staff, domestic violence centers, and the church (e.g., church leaders, spiritual advisors, mentors, and counselors).

Many people within the church wish to help their abused sisters in Christ but need help to understand how the abused woman feels, why she thinks the way she does, and what her internal conflicts are. Those who are trying to help a woman who is repeatedly abused often lose patience with her and stop asking questions or listening. Family and friends turn away and get tired of helping. She is told, "You're on your own now...." Her behaviors often appear irrational, but the reality is that she is trying to make sense of what is happening. She is confused about her husband's violent behavior. She wants answers, but she is in a state of shock and, therefore, has difficulty processing the information she needs to seek help. She usually is unaware that the violence has infected her own thinking and psychological wellbeing over time. When a woman finally realizes that she is a victim of domestic violence, she may already have been experiencing the physical and emotional effects of the violence.

Those who are trying to help the abused woman are likely to call what she is experiencing "domestic violence" before she does. She may see that her relationship has components of violence but not accept that she is a victim of "domestic violence." This label is embarrassing and degrading for many women, particularly those who are well-educated and think they "ought to know better."

Before a woman can seek change, however, she must accept that she is in an abusive relationship. Until she reaches this point, she will not be ready to take the necessary steps to change her situation. It is more important for her friends and family members to listen to her story again and again so that she can process what is happening to her. People who truly wish to help must also gain an in-depth understanding of how the abused woman thinks and feels. They must allow her to develop her own convictions about her need for change.

Myths about Domestic Violence

To effectively help the abused woman, the friends, family, and the faith community must evaluate their beliefs or perceptions about domestic violence. "There are many misconceptions, myths, and stereotypes about domestic abuse" that have become part of the culture.[1] Everyone absorbs or comes to believe some of these myths. Myths also lead to misconceptions about the abused woman among the people who are willing to help her, which may hinder them from helping her effectively.

The abused woman also has absorbed some of the myths about her abuse, which hinders her ability to change her situation. For example, she may believe that she has limited resources for seeking change.

Myths are difficult to change because they are a part of society's system of beliefs. Most societies have a high tolerance for abuse and/or a high level of denial. It is easier to accept these "beliefs" than to question and fight them. People who want to help the abused woman must evaluate the following myths and stereotypes.[2]

Myth #1: Domestic violence affects only a small percent of the population. Fact: Nearly one in four women in the United States reports experiencing violence by a current or former spouse or dating partner at some point in her life.³ An estimated 1.3 million women are victims of physical assault by an intimate partner each year.⁴

Various sources estimate that from one-quarter to one-half of all the women in the United States today have been or will be battered at some point in their lives. Estimates of abuse rates are difficult to obtain because most abuse likely goes unreported. It is embarrassing for many people to admit to abuse.

Myth #2: Domestic violence occurs only in poor, uneducated, and minority families. Fact: Studies have shown that domestic violence occurs in all types of families, regardless of income, educational level, ethnicity, or race. Abused women can include psychologists, doctors, nurses, even a president of a nation. Some might say, "I would never be a battered woman," or "That happens to other women, not me." The truth is any woman can be abused, even women who "ought to know better."

Myth #3: "If things get that bad, she must have done something to provoke it," or "It takes two to tango." Fact: Abused women often are blamed for the abuse. Some are labeled as "paranoid," "clingy," "emotionally or mentally unstable," "nagging," "codependent," or "relationship addicts." The abused woman also tends to blame herself. She might feel that she deserved the abuse.⁵ Nothing a woman does justifies physical assault or emotional degradation and humiliation. Abusers often abuse out of a deep-seated need for control and a sense of entitlement.

Myth #4: Abuse is caused by alcohol, drug abuse, stress, and mental illness. Fact: Alcohol and drug use may be used to calm the abuser's anxieties and give him a sense of power but are not the root of the abuse.⁶ The root cause is a need for control. Many acts of violence are committed when there is no evidence of alcohol or drug use. The abuse is not due to stress, especially not to stress on the job. If that were the case, his coworkers would be his victims.

Myth #5: She must like it or she would leave the relationship. Fact: Unfortunately, leaving an abusive relationship does not guarantee safety. Violence can continue and may even escalate after a woman leaves her partner. Abused women often make attempts to leave but are prevented from doing so due to factors such as financial dependence on the abuser, social isolation, or religious beliefs. Fear for her own safety is a legitimate concern among women attempting to leave an abusive relationship. Leaving the relationship may not guarantee safety. The violence may continue or escalate after the women leaves the relationship. [7]

Myth # 6: Domestic violence is none of my business. Abuse is a private matter. Fact: The Centers for Disease Control and Prevention estimates that the health-related costs of rape, physical assault, stalking, and homicide committed by intimate partners exceed $5.8 billion each year. Of that amount, nearly $4.1 billion is for direct medical and mental health care services. Domestic violence also is estimated to cost nearly $1.8 billion in lost productivity or wages in the United States.[8] Domestic violence is a family affair, a community affair, and a national affair. The fact that one in four women experiences domestic violence suggests that everyone knows someone who has been abused. This individual could be your mother, sister, aunt, friend, neighbor, or you.

Changing these myths is necessary to change perceptions about the abused woman's experiences and attitudes toward her as she seeks help.

How to Help

Members of the community who wish to help the abused woman must receive education to understand domestic violence and its effects on the lives of the woman and her family. Education also produces awareness of resources in the community. When domestic violence is disclosed or suspected, it is important to be aware of emergency shelters in the community, 24-hour crisis lines, counseling services, support groups, and legal assistance and court advocacy programs. Individuals can attend workshops, read books, or volunteer at shelters or domestic violence centers to learn how to effectively help abused women.

With proper education, a community member can be the abused woman's advocate by helping her file restraining orders or develop a safety plan. Community programs exist in many communities to assist with these activities and to help the abused woman implement her safety plan. Key elements of a safety plan (adapted from *Social*

Worker's Practice Guide to Domestic Violence, published by the Washington State Department of Social and Health Services) include:

- *Planning for immediate safety and safety during assaults.* This component of the plan might involve having access to a door for escape or moving away from the kitchen, bathroom, or areas where weapons are kept, during physical assaults. Or it might involve establishing a signal to let the neighbors and/or children know when to call 911.
- *Planning for escape.* This part of the plan might involve securing copies of or taking critical documents, for example, passport, green card, social security card, bank records, other financial records; children's birth certificates, passports, medical and schools records; and even pet vaccination records to a safe place outside the home. Small, valuable personal items and family heirlooms also can be moved to a safe place. Ideally, children might be sent away to "visit" relatives, and pets might be boarded elsewhere prior to the woman's planned escape.
- *Planning for long-term safety.* If the woman has left the relationship, her safety plan might involve changing the locks, changing her telephone number (unlisted), using blocks and caller ID, knowing what to do when being stalked, and working with her employer to ensure her safety at work.
- *Internet safety.* A safety plan also might involve blocking the perpetrator from tracking Internet activities.
- *Planning for emotional support.* The plan also should include strategies for coping with the emotional and physical effects of domestic violence. Identifying support groups in her area and participating in these groups for validation and support are essential for healing.
- *Planning for children's safety.* The safety plan should include measures such as providing information (in writing with necessary documentation) to schools, daycare centers, children's activity leaders, family, and friends about who is (and is not) allowed to pick up the children. She or her helper should contact the State Department to put a hold on her children's

passports. She should designate a safe location for the children that is near but outside of the home where they can go if they feel threatened or just need emotional support (e.g., a neighbor, family member, etc.).[9]

As stated earlier, it is important to refer the woman to professional community services that have the ability to protect her and her children. When there is potential for physical harm, it is important to stress to the abused woman that she cannot protect her life and the lives of the children alone. Encourage her to seek legal assistance. Many women may not want to file restraining orders because it is "just a piece of paper." However, documentation of violations of an order can build a case legally.

When the abused woman comes for help, listen to her with a nonjudgmental attitude and believe her. If her story provokes strong emotions in you or if you have difficulty believing her story, refer her to someone else. Help her to identify signs of violence in her relationship.

Provide educational material about domestic violence, but advise her not to share the materials with her abuser. Validate her feelings, as well as respecting her wishes and supporting her choices. Focus on her strengths and abilities. Offer physical support, such as helping with childcare. Offer your home as a safe haven. If she is in the process of legal proceedings related to child custody or separation/divorce, accompany her at court hearings.

The community also can hold abusers accountable for the abuse. There are laws that protect the victims. Be aware of those laws and use them to hold the abuser accountable. Unwillingness to take action against abusers may place the life of a woman and her children at risk.

In addition to helping individual abused women, individuals and groups can become involved in preventing domestic violence in their communities. Prevention is key to stopping domestic violence. One opportunity for prevention is premarital counseling in churches, for example.

Prevention also involves helping women gain an awareness of the characteristics of an abuser. Women who learn to identify the "red flags" for potential abuse will be better able to make informed decisions during the early phases of dating and certainly before they commit to marriage.

Below are some of the common red flags to spot potential abusers (some of these behaviors overlap with the behaviors described in the section on "Types of emotional and psychological abuse").

- *Routinely exhibits road rage/aggressive driving.* Blocking other drivers from passing him; using obscene gestures, aggressively honking, yelling out the window, and leaving the car to threaten other drivers; following/tailgating drivers who make him angry.
- *Blames former girlfriends for failed relationships.* He is involved in ongoing conflict with his ex about various issues.
- *Lacks respect for her privacy and personal boundaries.* He may call at odd hours "just to check in" or may just show up at her job or other places unannounced. This behavior is often initially mistaken for romantic behavior. He may justify this behavior by saying, "I can't be away from you," or, "I had to hear your voice."[10]
- *Rushes the relationship.* He gets attached very quickly and rushes through the getting-to-know-you phase of a courtship so that the woman will know little about his past or family. He may present this hurried behavior as romantic by saying, "I can't live without you," or, "I've never felt love like this with anyone." Potential abusers raise the idea of marriage early in the relationship or insist on moving in together. They are extremely emotionally dependent or needy early in the relationship. If she tries to slow things down, he will make her feel like she is overreacting.[11]
- *Makes decisions about social plans, dinner menus, etc. without consulting her.* He may not ask her what she wants or if his plans fit her schedule.
- *Exhibits excessive jealousy.* Shows jealousy of her interactions with friends, coworkers, and others who he imagines might threaten the relationships. He may present this behavior as proof of his love. He is suspicious of her activities that do not involve him. He may monopolize her time. He wants her

to spend all of her free time with him during the courtship. "If the jealousy is out of proportion with your innocent interactions with other people, that is a reason for concern. Such jealousy is not the result of an intense attraction to you or how desirable you may be to others. His jealousy is about insecurity and his need to control you."[12]

During premarital counseling, it is important to:
- Encourage the woman to observe the dynamics of Mr. Right's family and to ask his family members and friends about their relationship with him. Does he have deep, meaningful relationships with others? Family members may not want to verbalize their feelings. Observing his interaction with them, however, will provide indicators of possible future problems.
- Ask the women privately about any uncomfortable feelings she may have experienced during the courtship and explore these feelings with her.
- Ask how she resolves conflicts with her own family. How does this compare to the way he resolves conflicts with his family? Ask for recent examples of how she resolves conflicts within her own family and with her partner.
- Encourage longer dating to allow her to get to know him better.
- Most importantly, encourage her to trust her intuition. If something does not feel right, she should examine what it is. If she feels that her conscience is being violated, the relationship is not right!

How the Church Can Help

SUSAN

WHAT THE CHURCH CAN DO: Listen without judging the woman and provide a safe place emotionally. Help the woman process what she is feeling, but also encourage her to live by her convictions. Help her to stay centered on God and make her responses as she interacts in the relationship. Help the woman to forgive in order to guard her heart against bitterness. If the husband is Christian, exercise church discipline as appropriate. Encourage professional counseling individually before couple counseling and provide a safe place physically if and when needed.

REV. ZEKE WHARTON

CHURCHES CAN PROVIDE a variety of tangible means of support for a woman trying to escape or heal from an abusive situation. In one case, to make the adjustment to living on her own, the abused woman benefited from very practical acts of kindness by those in her church community—folks regularly mowed her grass, cooked her meals that could be stored in the freezer, and helped her create and manage a budget while she was dealing with the emotional consequences of abuse. In another situation, babysitting and a place to occasionally spend the night were the most strategic things that the church community could provide. Different people have different gifts they can bring to bear. When people, in true loving friendship and service, step forward to use their gifts, it makes an enormous difference.

When a woman comes to the church for help, she is experiencing physical, psychological, and spiritual abuse. Coming to the church means that she is beginning to open up about the relationship at home. It is important to recognize that a transformation has taken place within this woman. The abuse has had an effect on her thinking and perception. It also is equally important to note that she has made all the changes of which she is capable to change the situation. She has tried doing what her husband wants, maybe has received some secular counseling, and none of this has worked. It takes courage for this woman to come to the church for help. She comes seeking clarity, validation, and physical, psychological, and spiritual support. Asking for help, however, does not mean that she is ready to leave the marriage. On the other hand, she may be ready to leave and is seeking a support network.

She also is seeking clarification about what is happening in her marriage. Her story is not clear and is confusing to most people, including herself, because it constantly changes and does not make sense. She needs someone to believe the story even though, at times, it is fragmented. Nevertheless, she is telling the truth. She is not exaggerating. In fact, in most cases she is minimizing what is occurring at home. Remember she does not give full details about what is happening at home because it is embarrassing or it does not make sense to her. For example, it may seem crazy that he buys food for the kids, but if he is not home she is not to let them eat the food he bought. If a hungry kid happens to eat his food, she will have to reimburse him twice the original price. But that is the truth, because her husband does not behave rationally.

As she seeks clarity, she may not understand or may be in denial that she is in an abusive relationship. Or she may begin to recognize that something is wrong with the relationship but may not understand its impact. She may need to talk but not be ready to find solutions. She may talk about how bad the situation is but may not be ready to make a change. She needs time to process what is happening. This phase is difficult for most people because they want to find solutions. Listen to her story and believe her. Help her to find clarity. Ask open-ended questions. For example, ask her, "What are the facts?" "Does it make sense to you?"

She needs validation of her experience. Validation is the first step to empowerment. She wants someone to validate that her husband's behaviors are wrong and are negatively affecting the family. To help her, it is important to have an understanding of domestic violence and its impact. Wrong advice may reduce her ability to cope, weaken her ability to make decisions and seek the services she needs, and even put her life in danger. It is important to know the church's limitations. If you do not know how to help, please refer her to a Domestic Violence Center in your community. Domestic violence victim support groups are important to validate the woman's experience, help her feel less alone, and see how others have changed their situation.

Refer her to appropriate, local services outside the church if you have any concerns about safety, because these services offer the financial, legal, and protective resources that are necessary to ensure safety for her and her children.

As she begins to open up, ask her about safety. Safety should be the first priority when you begin to help the woman. Is her relationship safe? Can she trust him with her life? If she has any uncomfortable feelings regarding her safety or her children's safety, she also needs a safety plan.

Learn about the components of a safety plan. Help her develop this plan. Hold her accountable for following the plan. Do not encourage her to tell her husband about her plan, especially if she is contemplating leaving the relationship. Guide her to appropriate resources (e.g., from the police department, victims programs, crisis hot-lines, legal aid, shelters, social services, immigration, state department, etc.). Help her to navigate these resources.

Encourage her to believe in herself, to believe that she is capable of making the right choice. The power is in the choice. Emphasize her strengths. Reassure her that you are there to help her and will support her, regardless of whether she chooses to stay in the relationship or to leave.

EDITH

I CAN RECALL TWO powerful statements made by my sisters in Christ. The bearers of those statements were not aware of the impact of their words. The first statement was, "Whatever choice you make, we will support you." It meant the decision to leave or stay in my relationship was mine and they trusted that I was capable of making the right choice. They were going to be there for me. The second statement was, "I don't know how to help you."

I respected that statement. It made me realize that the church may not have the knowledge or resources to help me, and it was OK to find help in the community.

Meet the woman where she is in her faith. Use the scriptures to help her clarify negative concepts of God, rather than focusing on her sins. Help her to understand God's loving nature, first and foremost. Allow her to ask the hard questions. She may not want to reveal her anger or struggles with God, especially if she is speaking to a pastor. Encourage her to participate in a support group where she can express her true feelings toward God without fear of a critical response. Ultimately, she has to follow the scriptures and do what they say, but she must develop her own convictions and repent of her own free will. The scriptures have the power to convict her.

EDITH

I REMEMBER, on multiple occasions, describing events at home and my spiritual mentor asking a reflective question like "What do you think?" I had to go home and think before answering. If I had misconceptions about God, she would direct me to scriptures to read to help me develop my own convictions.

Teach that domestic violence is sin. Look at the sinful behaviors that are the characteristics of domestic violence. For example, deception, hostility, quarreling, jealousy, outbursts of anger, selfish ambition, and dissensions are characteristics of abusers (Galatians 5:21). The Bible is full of scriptures in which God condemns violence; Psalm 11:5–7, Ezekiel 7:11, and Malachi 2:16 are just a few examples. All of these sins separate us from God and require repentance.

Repentance is a change of heart, a complete turnaround. It is obvious and requires accountability. Paul says, "For godly sorrow brings repentance that leads to salvation and leaves no regret, but worldly sorrow brings death. See what this godly sorrow has produced in you: what earnestness, what eagerness to clear yourself, what indignation, what alarm, what concern, what readiness to see justice done" (2 Corinthians 7:10, NIV).

The abuser should demonstrate godly sorrow, particularly if he claims to be a Christian. Godly sorrow is demonstrated in indignation and alarm directed at himself because his abusive actions have destroyed his family. His repentance should begin with an enduring understanding of how he has deeply hurt his wife and God. An early sign of repentance is the husband admitting that he is an abuser and actively seeking help to change his abusive behaviors. He should be asking others to hold him accountable. If he only exhibits worldly sorrow, he has not repented. "Worldly sorrow" is when he says he is sorry only after having been exposed, facing legal consequences, or when she leaves him.

According to Marie Fortune in her book *Keeping The Faith*, "If your partner has truly repented and been converted, has genuinely turned to God, then he should perform acts worthy of his repentance. You should wait and watch for those acts; wait for him to no longer be abusive and controlling toward anyone."[13]

An abused woman should not be pushed toward premature forgiveness when there is no repentance or accountability on the part of her abuser. She needs time to go through the forgiveness process. Only God's Holy Spirit can help her do that. Some Christians may be more comfortable with the idea of instant forgiveness. True forgiveness, however, requires healing of emotional hurts, which takes time. In Matthew 18:15–18, Jesus taught forgiveness in the context of justice and healing. Jesus may have recognized that it is difficult to receive true forgiveness and healing if the person who inflicted the hurt refuses to repent. Separation from that person may be needed to start the forgiveness process.

Remember, do not recommend couples counseling because it is ineffective and it becomes a place to control the woman. Also, the woman may not expose the truth during the sessions due to fear of the husband's retaliation. It may endanger the life of the woman if the husband is physically violent. Get rid of the violence first. Individual counseling may be more effective because it allows the counselor to obtain a truthful version of the story from the woman and gain a better understanding of what is happening at home.

Help her to develop the conviction to speak the truth about every new incident of abuse to hold him accountable and help him to repent. The truth will set her free, as stated in John 8:32. Covering up his sin does not help him to change. In the biblical sense, she is his helpmate, but her goal is to help him make it to heaven, not hell.

Try to understand her spiritual dilemmas. Clarify that she is not responsible for the conversion of her husband. God has given all of us the freedom of choice. She can pray that he chooses God and changes but that choice is his, not hers.

Define what submission *is not*. Accepting physical, verbal, and sexual abuse is not submission in the biblical sense. Church leaders must emphasize that submission does not mean that one should accept physical or psychological abuse. Reinforce that these behaviors affect her psychological and spiritual wellbeing.

If you use Sarah as an example of a submissive wife, also focus on the mutual relationship she had with her husband. Abraham allowed his wife to participate in the decision-making process.

Sarah had a voice in the relationship. In Genesis 16, Sarah tells Abraham to sleep with her servant, Hagar. In Genesis 21, Sarah tells Abraham to send Hagar and her son away because she saw him "making fun" of her son Isaac. God tells Abraham to honor Sarah's request and takes responsibility for caring for Hagar and her son. Clearly, Sarah had a voice in her relationship with Abraham that abused women do not.

In 1 Samuel 26, Abigail had authority in the household and was able to mobilize resources to save her life and the lives of the members of her household. She did what was right to protect those in her care, regardless of her husband's behavior. This demonstrates that a Christian woman has a moral right and obligation to protect her own life, as well as the lives of those in her household, by seeking help from the law and the community. To help the abused woman develop the conviction to do what is right, stress the strength of will and character that Sarah and Abigail exhibited.

Distinguish her suffering from that of Jesus described in 1 Peter 2:21–23. Jesus' sufferings had a purpose. That purpose was to save us from our sins. The abused woman's suffering is not her cross to bear. It has no purpose but to encourage the sins of her husband. There are no examples in the scriptures that justify or support spousal violence. This kind of suffering is not God's will for women.

The role of the Christian community is to clarify the difference between voluntary suffering and involuntary or unjustified suffering. Their role is to protect the abused woman and her children. Encouraging the family to endure purposeless suffering leads to destruction of the family.

The woman's faith is crucial in the healing process; therefore, faith communities should help her build her faith and empower her by validating the fact that God has given her the power of choice to make right decisions. She has to reexamine her dilemma, make her peace with God, and reclaim His promises. She needs his wisdom and strength as she faces her abuse and seeks healing. If she does not do this, her relationship with God will fade away.

Key points to remember:

- When the woman comes to you for help, evaluate your beliefs about the male and female roles in a relationship.
- Know what domestic violence is. Know how to recognize behaviors of an abuser and techniques the abuser uses to control the woman's behavior.
- Know how to recognize common behaviors of women who have experienced domestic violence. Understand the effects of trauma and abuse, particularly within the marital relationship.
- Identify and debunk your own myths about domestic violence.

- Name his abusive behaviors as domestic violence. When violence enters a relationship and all the vows are broken, that relationship should not be considered a normal relationship anymore. The abused woman should not use normal relationships as a standard to evaluate her relationship.
- Realize that the stories about *marital* relationships in the scriptures were not described as violent or abusive. A violence-free relationship cannot be the guide for a violent relationship.
- Get rid of the violence before working on the relationship. As noted earlier, women experiencing violence may not be able to properly process information, due to the psychological effects of the violence. They also will feel confused and trapped when given tactics that might work with normal, reasonable husbands, but not with violent and controlling men.
- Don't use statement like "It takes two to tango," or, "What was your role?" That means, "What did you do to cause him to abuse you?" No one deserves to be abused. Nothing someone does should justify a physical assault or emotional degradation and humiliation.
- Understand that the woman has to come to God for repentance by opening up about her abuse. One of her sins is covering up her abuse. Continuing to allow her husband to abuse her without accountability, especially if he is a Christian, is a sin.
- Don't advise communication to improve the relationship. An abusive man will use communication as a weapon of manipulation and control, not as a tool for reconciliation and understanding.
- Listen and don't prejudge or stereotype. If the woman realizes you are judging or not listening, she may stop confiding in you.
- Don't relate the husband's abuse to his anger. Yes, he has anger, but this is not the root cause of his abuse. His abuse is primarily done to control the woman.
- Recognize that anger management classes may not be an effective way to stop the violence.
- When talking about forgiveness, don't assume that the woman is holding onto old hurts and can't let them go. She may have

forgiven every past hurt in her relationship, but she experiences a continually revolving door of hurts and increasingly short respites from the pain.
- Understand that his abusive actions are not due to stress, especially not to stress on the job. If that were the case, as stated earlier, his coworkers would be his victims.
- Do not hesitate to refer the woman to secular resources that she needs. The secular community offers important legal, medical, and other professional resources to ensure the woman's safety and protection of her family and resources. Most churches simply do not have the resources to provide the myriad types of help that an abused woman may require. Debunk all the myths that the secular community will discourage her from following her faith. Respect her as a thinking adult who can stand on her own convictions.
- Focus on spiritual healing and social support of the woman and her children. Remember that, as a Christian, this woman already has an advantage: God will heal her. Your role is to help her understand and receive God's love and spiritual healing. As you help her to strengthen her faith, she will develop a strong conviction and have the power to make the right decisions.

CHAPTER 9

SEXUAL VIOLENCE AGAINST WOMEN IN THE BIBLE AND HOW THE COMMUNITY RESPONDED

There are no stories about *marital* relationships in the scriptures that are described as violent or abusive; however, the Bible is not without examples of the community taking action to defend women who were victims of violence. The Bible stories discussed in this chapter deal with sexual assault. Sexual assault or rape is one of the tactics the abuser uses to achieve and maintain control and is prevalent in domestic violence relationships.

The purpose of these stories is to illustrate how the biblical community responded to sexual violence against women. The families and the community held those who perpetrated the violence accountable for their actions.

As we examine the scriptures, we will find that the thoughts and attitudes exhibited by families and communities in response to acts of violence against women have not changed since biblical times. Women were considered property of men, which is still the case in many countries today. Even in developed countries, victims of rape and domestic violence frequently find that they have little or no voice. And perpetrators around the world still feel that is their right and privilege to control women to get what they want or feel they deserve. In addition, the woman often is blamed for the violence. In the case of sexual assault, she may be told that her dress, body movement, or behavior invited the assault.

The response to perpetrators in biblical times does appear to differ from the response we see in modern times. Family members in the Bible do not sit back and pretend that the violence has not occurred. The woman may have no power to seek retribution, but someone in the family usually does on her behalf. The Bible stories presented in this section show how the perpetrators paid for their crime with their lives. In one story, the family member even brought the case before the nation and a refusal to hand over the perpetrators led to civil war.

It is important to note that the nature of the violence against the women in these stories is not an accepted behavior by God's people. It violates the woman, the family, and God's laws. As part of God's people, we too have the moral responsibility and are called *to respond* to stop violence against women and hold the perpetrators accountable for their acts of violence.

Dinah

Genesis 34:1–31 tells the story of Dinah, who was abused by Shechem, son of the local tribal ruler. "Now Dinah, the daughter Leah had borne to Jacob, went out to visit the women of the land. When Shechem son of Hamor the Hittite, the ruler of that area, saw her, he took her and raped her" (verses 1–2, NIV). When Dinah went to visit her girlfriends in the area, Shechem, the local prince, did not waste any time with wooing.

"His heart was drawn to Dinah daughter of Jacob; he loved the young woman and spoke tenderly to her" (verse 3). How can he love her when he just raped her? It was more lust than love. Or, was he attempting to cover up the sin he had committed? If he loved her as he claimed, he should have persuaded her to become his wife within the standards and traditions of her culture.

Later, his tone changed from speaking tenderly to her to entitlement. He said to his father, Hamor, in verse 4, "Get me this girl as my wife." It sounded more like a command, as if to say, "I am the prince; you can't deny me what I want." Abusers have the same sense of entitlement: "This is my right ... I can do what I want" and "I want it now."

The Family Response

Genesis 34:5 continues, describing the family's response. "When Jacob heard that his daughter Dinah had been defiled, his sons were in the fields with his livestock; so he did nothing about it until they came home." He didn't ask any questions or make a statement. He didn't talk to his daughter. Was he afraid of the local leaders, or, losing his standing in the community?

Then Shechem's father, Hamor, went out to talk with Jacob and to discuss the marriage proposal, as his son had commanded him (verse 6). Verse 7 states: "Meanwhile, Jacob's sons had come in from the fields as soon as they heard what had happened. They were shocked and furious, because Shechem had done an outrageous thing in Israel by sleeping with Jacob's daughter—a thing that should not be done." I wonder if, had the brothers arrived after Jacob's conversation with Hamor, Jacob would have agreed to the proposal.

Shechem had done a disgraceful thing against Jacob's family, a thing that should never have been done! What a crime! Rape wasn't an accepted behavior. The rape violated not only God's laws but would have dishonored Dinah and her family within that culture. Jacob, the head of the family, did nothing, so the brothers took matters into their own hands. Something had to be done because of what Shechem had done to their sister. They refused to sit back like their father and pretend that nothing had happened. They understood that Shechem should pay a price for committing such a hideous crime.

Once the brothers showed up at the meeting with Hamor, the discussion turned back to business. "But Hamor said to them, 'My son Shechem has his heart set on your daughter. Please give her to him as his wife. Intermarry with us; give us your daughters and take our daughters for yourselves. You can settle among us; the land is open to you. Live in it, trade in it, and acquire property in it'" (verses 8–10). The basic proposal was that their people could intermarry and be one big family. Hamor's and Jacob's families (tribes) could do business and Jacob's family would become wealthy among the Hittites.

Why didn't Hamor offer that proposal before his son lusted after Dinah? It appears he was attempting to fix things quickly to cover up the crime his son had committed against Jacob's family. Out of desperation, Shechem expanded his proposal to Dinah's father and brothers, "Let me find favor in your eyes, and I will give you whatever you ask. Make the price for the bride and the gift I am to bring as great as you like, and I'll pay whatever you ask me. Only give me the young woman as my wife" (verses 11–12).

The brothers' response at first was shock. Wait a minute; isn't this about rape? Our sister was raped. We have been disgraced and now you want us to let our sister marry your son? Genesis 34:13–14 states, "Because their sister Dinah had been defiled, Jacob's sons replied deceitfully as they spoke to Shechem and his father Hamor. They said to them, 'We can't do such a thing; we can't give our sister to a man who is not circumcised. That would be a disgrace to us.'"

Perhaps after processing Shechem's and his father's offer, the brothers might have realized that the proposal presented a way for them to achieve their goal of retribution. They agreed to talk business, but on one condition, according to verses 15–18: "We will enter into an agreement with you on one condition only: that you become like us by circumcising all your males. Then we will give you our daughters and take your daughters for ourselves. We'll settle among you and become one people with you. But if you will not agree to be circumcised, we'll take our sister and go."

Meanwhile, Dinah, the victim, became the object of a business transaction with no input of her own. She had no voice. No one asked how she was feeling or coping. Just as it is today, when a woman reports violence against her, her voice often is taken away by the legal system and her dignity is lost. She has to explain the events to not just one person but to layers of people, from policemen to hospital workers to social workers to judges, as she goes through the system. As she experiences this process, her soul is exposed. Yet at the same time, she becomes invisible. Her thoughts and feelings don't matter anymore. She becomes an object (i.e., her body becomes a piece of evidence, she is simply a witness for the prosecution).

Hamor was so controlled by his son that he was willing to do anything to help fulfill Shechem's selfish desire. So Hamor took the proposal to the town council:

Their proposal seemed good to Hamor and his son Shechem. The young man, who was the most honored of all his father's family, lost no time in doing what they said, because he was delighted with Jacob's daughter. So Hamor and his son Shechem went to the gate of their city to speak to the men of their city.

"These men are friendly toward us," they said. "Let them live in our land and trade in it; the land has plenty of room for them. We can marry their daughters and they can marry ours. But the men will agree to live with us as one people only on the condition that our males are circumcised, as they themselves are. Won't their livestock, their property, and all their other animals become ours? So let us agree to their terms, and they will settle among us. (Genesis 34:18–23, NIV)

The Message version reads, "This is a very good deal for us—these people are very wealthy with great herds of livestock and we're going to get our hands on it. So let us do what they ask and let them settle down with us." Hamor persuaded his people to accept the proposal by emphasizing the financial gain. All the men who went out of the city gate agreed with Hamor and his son Shechem, and every male in the city was circumcised" (verse 24).

Then, the plan for revenge was executed:

Three days later, while all of them were still in pain, two of Jacob's sons, Simeon and Levi, Dinah's brothers, took their swords and attacked the unsuspecting city, killing every male. They put Hamor and his son Shechem to the sword and took Dinah from Shechem's house and left. The sons of Jacob came upon the dead bodies and looted the city where their sister had been defiled. They seized their flocks and herds and donkeys and everything else of theirs in the city and out in the fields. They carried off all their wealth and all their women and children, taking as plunder everything in the houses. (Genesis 34: 25–29, NIV)

However, afterward, (verse 30), Jacob rebuked his sons Simeon and Levi: "You have brought trouble on me by making me obnoxious to the

Canaanites and Perizzites, the people living in this land. We are few in number, and if they join forces against me and attack me, I and my household will be destroyed." Jacob's primary focus was his reputation. His daughter was never his focus. He was focused on how everyone around him would view him and come after him. But despite his misgivings, no one came to destroy his family. Instead, his family became the foundation of God's people.

The brothers argued with their father (verse 31), "Should he have treated our sister like a prostitute?" Dinah's brothers may not have behaved in a just or righteous way when they took the law into their own hands, but they understood that a crime had been committed. Retribution was needed and they did something! The price was high and a whole community of people was killed, including the perpetrator. In our modern age, the community can advocate for laws that will hold perpetrator accountable for sexual crimes.

This story demonstrates that God's people understood that a man who assaulted a woman had to pay the consequences of his actions and could not cover them up by forcing marriage.

Shechem did not acknowledge that he had committed a crime. Instead, he appeared to think that putting forth an honorable request to marry his victim excused his behavior. His behavior parallels the behaviors of abusive men today who think it is their right and privilege to inflict violence against women, especially their wives.

Tamar

Tamar's story begins with Amnon, desperate and obsessively in love with his sister, Tamar: "In the course of time, Amnon son of David fell in love with Tamar, the beautiful sister of Absalom son of David. Amnon became so obsessed with his sister Tamar that he made himself ill. She was a virgin, and it seemed impossible for him to do anything to her" (2 Samuel 13:1–2, NIV).

His sickness might have been due to his lust and subsequent frustration at not being able to satisfy that lust. Laws forbade having sex with a virgin unless you were married to her. Laws described in Leviticus 18:9 also stated, "Do not have sex with your sister, whether she is your father's daughter or your mother's daughter, whether she was born in the same house or elsewhere" (*The Message*).

"Now Amnon had an adviser named Jonadab, son of Shimeah, David's brother. Jonadab was a very shrewd man. He asked Amnon, 'Why do you, the king's son, look so haggard morning after morning? Won't you tell me?'" Amnon told him his desire for his sister. "I'm in love with Tamar, my brother Absalom's sister" (2 Samuel 13:3, NIV). So, Amnon's buddy helped him devise a plan to get what he wanted. After all, Amnon was the king's son, and Amnon believed it was his right and privilege to get he wanted, even if it involved manipulation or force. As described in 2 Samuel 13: 5–6, Jonadab told Amnon to fake illness and go to bed. "When the king came to see him, Amnon should say to him, 'I would like my sister Tamar to come and make some special bread in my sight, so I may eat from her hand.'" Amnon was so overcome with lust that he was willing to deceive his father. He also likely knew the laws described in Leviticus, but he was willing to violate God's law.

What were the king's thoughts when Amnon verbalized his request? Did he wonder how his son's watching someone cook his food and then feed him could cure his son's illness? In addition, Amnon already had servants to cook for him. Did the king wonder why Amnon was asking a daughter of the king to cook like a common servant? David's love for his firstborn son, his heir according to Jewish custom, may have hindered him from suspecting the bad motive behind his son's senseless request. In any event, King David granted the request and sent word to Tamar at the palace to go to Amnon's house and cook for him. Obediently, Tamar did as she was told (2 Samuel 13:7–8).

What might Tamar have been thinking? Did she think that it didn't make sense to have her brother watch her cook? Did she not recognize that his request had sexual hidden motives? She may have loved and trusted her brother or may have felt privileged to serve the heir. Amnon, on the other hand, preyed on his sister by violating her trust. He manipulated her just as today's perpetrators of sexual abuse prey on their victims' innocent love and trust and then inflict violence on them.

After Tamar prepared the food, "She took the pan and served him the bread, but he refused to eat. 'Send everyone out of here,' Amnon said. So everyone left him. Then Amnon said to Tamar, 'Bring the food here into my bedroom so I may eat from your hand.' And Tamar took the bread she had prepared and brought it to her brother Amnon in his bedroom" (2 Samuel 13:9–10, NIV).

Wait a minute! Didn't he watch her cook the food in the presence of others? Why was he requesting to eat in the bedroom? She followed his instructions without a clue that he had an ulterior motive. In the bedroom, while she was attempting to feed him, he grabbed her and said, "Come to bed with me my sister" (verse 11).

"No, my brother!" she replied. Then she pleaded with him by reminding him of God's laws and the severity of the sin: "Such a thing should not be done in Israel! Don't do this wicked thing!" (verse 12). Such a crime violated God's law and should not be tolerated by God's people. He did not listen to her plea.

Tamar made a second attempt to plead with Amnon by reminding him of the effects of his actions. She asks, "What about me? Where could I get rid of my disgrace?" Tamar is acknowledging that she will have to bear the shame of this sin before others. Her prospects of marriage also will be destroyed because she no longer will be a virgin. "And what about you? You will be called the greatest fool in all of Israel" (verse 13). Tamar is explaining that everyone will know that Amnon raped his own sister and this will disgrace him and the family. When he still does not respond to her pleas, she again attempts to persuade him to reconsider his actions and says, "Please speak to the king; he will not keep me from being married to you."

That seems like a great proposal for Amnon. After all, wasn't he obsessively in love with her? At that moment the true motive for his behaviors is exposed. He isn't in love with his sister, but in lust with her and wants sex.

Overcome with lustful passion for her, he ignores her pleas. Amnon "... refused to listen and since he was stronger than her, he raped her" (verse 14). This scripture implies that Tamar physically fought back. Where was everyone? Didn't they hear her scream? There had to be people around. A few minutes ago weren't they watching her cook? Didn't Amnon instruct them to leave? Someone should have heard her scream, but no one came to her rescue.

Tamar did everything to stop the rape by pleading and physically fighting back, but in the end she could do nothing to prevent her rape. What a horrible experience! Sexual abuse victims, as well as domestic violence victims, can relate to Tamar's sense of powerlessness because their perpetrators, too, have assaulted them despite their best efforts to stop the violence.

After he raped her, Amnon hated Tamar with intense hatred. In fact, he hated her more than he had loved her (verse 15). Did Amnon know what love was? His perception of love was based on sexual fantasy. Love doesn't lead someone to physically and sexually attack the object of his love.

Amnon saw Tamar lying there crying, bruised, bleeding, and frightened. He did not want to face his conscience. He did not want a reminder of his sin. So, in his mind, he may have shifted the blame on Tamar for "making him do it," for being pretty so that he sexually fantasized about her.

Amnon said to her, "'Get up and get out of my sight!' She said to him, 'Oh no, my brother, please don't send me away. You will damage me more than you have already done.' But he refused to listen to her. He called his personal servant and said, 'Get this woman out of my sight and bolt the door after her.' So his servant put her out and bolted the door after her. She was wearing an ornate robe, for this was the kind of garment the virgin daughters of the king wore. Tamar put ashes on her head and tore the ornate robe she was wearing. She put her hands on her head and went away, weeping aloud as she went" (2 Samuel 13:15–19, NIV).

Tamar wasn't afraid to expose what had happened to her. Tamar tore her robe and jewelry that indicated she was a virgin. She placed ashes on her head and cried out loud for all to see and hear what had happened. She wanted her family and the community to know that she had been wronged. No one responded except her brother, Absalom.

The Family Response

When Absalom heard about Tamar's rape, his response wasn't emotionally helpful. He asked, "Has that Amnon, your brother, been with you? Be quiet for now, my sister; he is your brother. Don't take this thing to heart" (2 Samuel 13:20, NIV). He acknowledged the rape but told his sister to keep it quiet. Act like nothing happened. Get over it. After all, he is your brother, too.

This kind of response can be seen in families in which there is physical, or sexual abuse by family members. Family members frequently encourage abuse victims to be quiet. "Don't tell anyone or the family will be harmed," or "No one will believe you," are common responses. Some family members of victims of domestic abuse will encourage women not to call the police or press charges. They may say, "I went through the same thing," or, "That's how men are." Absalom took Tamar to live with him. 2 Samuel 13: 22 notes that "Absalom never said a word to Amnon, either good or bad; he hated Amnon because he had disgraced his sister Tamar." The family never talks about this incident with Tamar again. She never recovers from the crime her brother committed against her and lives a depressed and isolated life.

In 2 Samuel 13:21 the story continues: "King David heard about what had happened and was furious," but did nothing. He didn't talk to his daughter to ask her about what her brother did or offer physical or emotional support. There is no mention of him confronting his son about the crime he committed against the family or disciplining his son for the evil he had committed against his sister. Amnon violated God's laws and King David protected him from facing the consequences of his sin. Many families today also protect perpetrators from the consequences of their actions. They do not hold the perpetrators accountable or help the victims.

There was no consequence for Amnon's actions. Tamar had no voice in seeking retribution for the crime against her. Her father did not assist her in implementing justice. Her only advocate was her brother. Amnon had to pay a price, so Absalom plotted to make his brother pay for raping his sister. Two years later, according to 2 Samuel 13:28–29, Absalom had a party and asked his father that his brothers attend. At the party Amnon was "high in spirits from drinking wine" when Absalom ordered his servants to kill him.

Jonadab, the man who helped Amnon formulate the plan to rape Tamar, was the bearer of the news of Amnon's death to the king in 2 Samuel 13:32–33. He said to the king, "This has been Absalom's expressed intention ever since the day Amnon raped his sister Tamar." I wonder how Jonadab felt? He neglected to mention his role in plotting Tamar's rape. Did he feel any remorse or feel responsible for Tamar's rape and Amnon's death? What about King David? I wonder how he felt when he was reminded of Absalom's reason for killing his brother? Did he have regrets for not holding Amnon accountable for his crime?

King David lost two sons that day. Absalom ran away and did not see his father for three years (2 Samuel 13:38–39). The king "longed" to see Absalom, for he had gotten over Amnon's death. Absalom did return home, but his relationship with his father was never the same. In the end, he revolted against his father and was killed.

Absalom committed a crime in murdering his brother, an act many may not agree with. What other options did he have to seek retribution for his sister? After all, King David, his father, was the most powerful man in the land. One can infer that Absalom might not have had the power to go after his brother through the legal process. However, Absalom was willing to risk everything to seek revenge for his sister, even if it meant breaking the law, destroying his relationship with his father, and losing his inheritance.

In our families and communities today, those in power continue to fail to protect and obtain retribution (i.e. prison) for victims of rape and domestic abuse. It is easier to pretend that the violence did not occur than to expose the violence and face the consequences.

Family and community members today should be advocates for members who are victims of violence. Unlike biblical times, today there are laws to help protect the victim, but a woman needs someone to advocate for her when her voice is taken away by the violence. That advocate can be a family member, a church member, a friend, or concerned member of the community.

Protecting the woman starts within the family, but some women are abandoned or neglected by their families and need outside support. Family members should be expected to hold perpetrators accountable, even if that perpetrator is a member of their own family. The community and church can support families in facing perpetrators, supporting and protecting victims, and exposing violence.

The Levite and His Concubine

It was an era when there was no king in Israel. A Levite, living as a stranger in the backwoods hill country of Ephraim, got himself a concubine, a woman from Bethlehem in Judah. But she quarreled with him and left, returning to her father's house in Bethlehem in Judah. She was there four months. Then her husband decided to go after her and try to win her back. He had a servant and a pair of donkeys with him. When he arrived at her father's house, the girl's father saw him, welcomed him, and made him feel at home. His father-in-law, the girl's father, pressed him to stay. He stayed with him three days; they feasted and drank and slept. (Judges 19:1–4, *The Message*)

On the fourth day the Levite was ready to leave, but his father-in-law persuaded him to stay another day: "But this time the man wasn't willing to spend another night. He got things ready, left, and went as far as Jebus (Jerusalem) with his pair of saddled donkeys, his concubine, and his servant. At Jebus, though, the day was nearly gone" (verses 10–11). As they progressed on their journey home, it became dark and they needed a place to rest.

The servant suggested that they spend the night in the city of the Jebusites (verse 11). The man replied, "No. We won't go into any city whose people are not Israelites. We will go on to Gibeah" (verse 12). He wanted to spend the night with the people of God. They finally arrived at Gibeah, or Ramah, which was land of the tribe of Benjamin, one of the twelve tribes of Israel. The group of travelers followed tradition by sitting in the city square to let everyone know that they were visitors and needed a place to stay; however, no one offered them any hospitality (verse 15). This was their first indication that the inhabitants of this city were not religious at all. They had drifted away from the rules of hospitality that their forefathers had practiced.

Finally, an old man from another city, who had moved to Ramah, was willing to show them hospitality. The man asked, "'Where are you going? Where did you come from?' The Levite replied, 'We are on our way from Bethlehem in Judah to a remote area in the hill country of

Ephraim where I live. I have been to Bethlehem in Judah and now I am going to the house of the Lord. No one has taken me in for the night. We have both straw and fodder for our donkeys and bread and wine for ourselves your servants—me, the woman, and the young man with us. We don't need anything'" (Judges 19:16–18, *The Message*).

It is interesting that he did not state that he had come to Bethlehem to get his wife. Wasn't that the reason for his trip? Nor did he state that the woman with him was his wife or concubine.

He also said that he was on his way to the house of the Lord, which does not seem to be the case. Perhaps he thought the old man would be more willing to help a religious man.

The Levite and his party went to spend the night at the old man's house. "While they were enjoying themselves, wicked men from the city surrounded the house. Pounding on the door, they shouted to the old man who owned the house, 'Bring out the man who came to your house so we can have sex with him'" (verse 22, NIV).

The people of God were more evil than those in the neighboring towns the Levite had made an effort to avoid. It might have been shocking for the Levite to hear what the men were requesting. This was the tribe of Benjamin, a part of God's people, and they were demanding to have sex with him, which is against God's law. The old man went outside and said to them, "No, my friends, don't be so vile. Since this man is my guest, don't do this outrageous thing. Look, here is my virgin daughter and his concubine. I will bring them out to you now, and you can use them and do to them whatever you wish. But as for this man, don't do such an outrageous thing" (Judges 19:23–24, NIV).

The old man knew how despicable it was to commit such a crime, yet he was willing to sacrifice his virgin daughter and the Levite's concubine, allowing them to do whatever they wished to the women. While the host would allow them to physically abuse and gang rape a female guest and a young virgin daughter, he would protect the man, also his guest, from this violence. What were the women's thoughts as the old man expressed his solutions to the crowd?

I assume that they felt that the old man and the Levite, in order to spare their own lives, were treating the women like helpless objects, sacrificing them instead of protecting them. It is painful for compassionate and moral people to imagine this situation today, but similar situations occur in abusive households around the world, where a man may prostitute his own wife or daughter for personal financial gain.

The men from the city refused the old man's offer. They kept demanding that the Levite come out. To save himself, the Levite pushed his concubine outside and "they raped her and abused her throughout the night, and at dawn they let her go. At daybreak the woman went back to the house where her master was staying, fell down at the door and lay there until daylight" (verses 25–26).

The Levite got up the next morning "to continue on his way." Was he planning to leave without this concubine if she hadn't come back to the house? When he opened the door, "there lay his concubine, fallen in the doorway of the house, with her hands on the doorstep." It must have been a horrible sight to see his wife lying by the doorstep, bleeding, bruised, swollen, and her body exposed like a deer hit by a car. One can only imagine how disfigured and pitiable she looked after the violence she had experienced. "He said to her, 'Get up; let's go.' But there was no answer." The woman was dead, so he placed her body on the donkey and left for home (verses 27–28).

"When he reached home, he took a knife and cut up his concubine, limb by limb, into twelve parts and sent them into all the areas of Israel" (verse 29). Maybe the decision to dismember her and send her body parts to the twelve tribes of Israel was the result of having walked with the woman's dead body on the donkey all the way home and the realization that he had used his wife as a sacrifice to save his own life. All these possible thoughts might have provoked his conscience to do something.

"Everyone who saw it was saying to one another, 'Such a thing has never been seen or done, not since the day the Israelites came up out of Egypt. Just imagine! We must do something! So speak up!'" (verse 30). It might have been a horrific experience to receive body parts but that awakened the conscience of the people to mobilize and do something to hold the abusers accountable.

The Community Response

Then all Israel from Dan to Beersheba and from the land of Gilead came together as one and assembled before the Lord in

Mizpah. The leaders of all the people of the tribes of Israel took their places in the assembly of God's people, four hundred thousand men armed with swords. (The Benjamites heard that the Israelites had gone up to Mizpah.) Then the Israelites said, "Tell us how this awful thing happened." (Judges 20:1–3, NIV).

The Levite explained, "During the night the men of Gibeah came after me and surrounded the house, intending to kill me. They raped my concubine, and she died" (verse 5). So he left out some "minor" details about his role in the violence. The Levite explained his later actions: "I took my concubine, cut her into pieces and sent one piece to each region of Israel's inheritance, because they committed this lewd and outrageous act in Israel" (verse 6). He demanded a response: "Now, all you Israelites speak up and tell me what you have decided to do" (verse 7). What are you going to do?

The people's moral conscience was aroused; everyone agreed that no one would leave until a decision had been made. In Judges 20:8–11, the Israelites are quoted as agreeing, "None of us will go home. No, not one of us will return to his house. But now this is what we'll do to Gibeah: when the army arrives at Gibeah in Benjamin, it can give them what they deserve for this outrageous act done in Israel." The people of Israel united that day to make the Benjamites pay for their act of violence.

Judges 20:12–13 continues, "The tribes of Israel sent messengers throughout the tribe of Benjamin, saying, 'What about this awful crime that was committed among you? Now turn those wicked men of Gibeah over to us so that we may put them to death and purge the evil from Israel,'" but the Benjamites refused. Many societies still refuse to hold perpetrators accountable for the violence they inflict against women. The leaders of the tribe of Benjamin knew that the men were guilty, yet they refused to prosecute them and were willing to go to war and sacrifice more lives (Judges 20:15–16).

The Benjamites had a strong army and won the first battle. After losing the first day, the Israelites had doubts about the decision to go to battle against their countrymen. They went back to God, weeping, and asked, "'Shall we go up again to fight against the Benjamites, our fellow

Israelites?' The Lord answered, 'Go up against them'" (Judges 20:23, NIV). God confirmed that they made the right choice in attempting to make the Benjamites pay for their crime. They needed that reassurance to empower them to fight back. An example was to be set that such evil would not be tolerated, especially among God's people.

In the end, the Israelites won. All the Benjamites' towns and property were destroyed, and only 600 men survived by running and hiding in the forest. The children and the women were spared (Judges 20:45–48). The entire community almost was destroyed because the leaders of the Benjamites had refused to hold the perpetrators accountable!

This story demonstrates that God sees the murder and rape of a single woman as very important. An entire country had to unite and go to war to send the message that such violence wasn't tolerated and had consequences. There was a crime and the perpetrators were to be punished. Refusing to punish the perpetrators wasn't an option and there were consequences for the leaders who refused to act.

Conclusion

It will take unity within the communities to stop violence against women. It is essential that the church work with secular domestic violence organizations to help Christian women who are victimized by violence. Each group has specific roles in preventing and stopping violence against women. Secular organizations can provide physical protection, legal and financial help, and professional counseling necessary for the survivor of violence and her children to return to normal lives. The Christian woman's faith should be respected as she seeks assistance within the secular community. The church's role is to hold its male members accountable for their abusive actions. The church should be a place where the silence about domestic violence is broken and where emotional and spiritual healing for the victims is provided. Another role of the church is to provide a physically and emotionally safe environment for the victim and her children.

Stopping the violence against women and holding perpetrators accountable starts within the family and continues within the community and society as a whole. The community can no longer sit back and watch its mothers, sisters, and daughters continue to endure violence. The church community must acknowledge the violence that is occurring in its congregation. The community at large and the society are morally obligated to take the responsibility to protect the woman and her children from violence.

Individually, we all have a moral responsibility to stop violence against women. *What are you going to do?* Helen Keller is often quoted as having said, "I am only one. But still I am one. I cannot do everything, but still I can do something. I will not refuse to do the something I can."

Some Facts about Sexual Assault within Marriage

Sexual assault or rape is one of the tactics used in violent relationships to establish control. "Rape in marriage is an extremely prevalent form of sexual violence, especially in relationships where there is physical violence. Studies using clinical samples of battered women reveal that between one-third and one-half of battered women are raped by their partners at least once."[1]

Another study estimated that rape occurs in up to 70 percent of relationships where there is domestic violence.[2] "Many women who are victims of marital rape have difficulty admitting to being raped. A wife who has been raped may question her right to refuse sexual intercourse with her husband."[3] Even though a woman may realize that she has been raped, it is easier to deny this fact than admit it to others.

In addition, traditional societal roles for a wife and, historically, laws that supported the rights of a husband to have sexual intercourse with his wife, make it difficult to prosecute the husband when he is guilty of rape. Only in recent years were laws implemented to make marital rape a crime. In the United States on July 5, 1993, marital rape was made a crime in all 50 states.[4] In the United Kingdom, marital rape was made a criminal act in 1991. Up until then it was considered impossible for a man to rape or sexually assault his wife. To quote: "A husband cannot rape his wife unless the parties are separated or the court has by injunction forbidden him to interfere with his wife or he has been given an undertaking in court not to interfere with her."[5]

AFTERWORD

The Word of God has amazing power to change and heal. It can serve as a catalyst for changing perceptions of the most horrific experiences of one's life. During those difficult times, when we rely on God and stay obedient to his Word, he transforms those weakest moments into amazing strength and growth.

This book was initially inspired by my personal struggle as a Christian woman experiencing domestic violence. I began to write while working through my own healing process, journaling and telling my story, and searching through the scriptures and other resources to find clarity and healing. One of the most empowering scriptures during my healing was Isaiah 9:6, "For to us a child is born, to us a son is given, and the government will be on his shoulder, And he will be called Wonderful Counselor, Mighty God, Everlasting Father, Prince of Peace" (NIV). This discovery has been the core of my healing process and the foundation on which this book stands. Christ is the ultimate healer, therapist, advocate, protector, encourager, the bearer of good news and peace.

I developed much of the formal material in this book in an attempt to guide and support other abused Christian women who participated in the support groups I led. I continued the writing beyond the support groups in the hope that many more Christian women could be reached and obtain freedom from the bondage of domestic violence.

This book, however, is not intended to serve on its own as an instructional manual for domestic violence, but as a supplementary tool for helping the Christian woman who has experienced, or is experiencing, spousal abuse. Although all relationships that involve domestic violence have similarities, every woman has a different story and responds to that experience in her own way. Her unique values, beliefs, culture, personality, past experiences, environment, and current strengths and limitations all influence how she responds to domestic violence. She therefore must find her own path toward healing.

As part of the community that attempts to support abused women, we must try to refrain from passing judgment or determining what is right or wrong for any individual woman. Aside from doing what we can to ensure the immediate safety of the abused woman and her children, we cannot act for her or make decisions for her. We can only offer unconditional support, guidance when it is requested, help when it is needed, and above all else, the unceasing love and mercy that was modeled by Jesus Christ. My hope is this book can help members of the faith community provide these types of assistance in the most effective way possible.

For those of us who have been or currently are in an abusive relationship, we must understand that no one person or even group of people can rescue us or meet all of our needs for emotional and spiritual healing. In the end, we must bring our struggles to the God of love and trust him to be our rescuer and our strength. Christ can play all of the distinct roles listed in Isaiah 9:6 as we individually seek to understand, heal, and break free from the bondage of domestic abuse. Christ can give the wisdom we need to make right choices. He can act as a father to guide us on the right path and be our defender as we seek support and justice from our community. Also, he can give us encouragement to help us stand firm in our faith, strength for our inner most spirit, and hope that our situation can change.

We also must make, accept responsibility for, and live with our own decisions. There will be consequences for whatever decision we make—especially the decision to take no action/make no change. This book is designed to help us work through some of our fears, develop or regain our trust in our God, evaluate our situation, make decisions that we can live with, and ultimately achieve the true emotional and spiritual freedom and healing that Christ offers us.

The reality is that stopping domestic violence is an enormous task for individuals or organizations. A team approach is needed. The family, church, government, and secular communities all have roles they can play in helping the victims and stopping the violence by holding

Afterword

the abusers accountable. We each have individual roles as we embark on this difficult task. For those of us who have conquered domestic violence, our role is to lead other victims of abuse to Christ.

The call to make a difference in the lives of other Christian domestic violence victims is seen in lives of the women who shared the most painful moments of their lives in this book to help others understand that God's Word is the transformer. During the most difficult times of their lives, they held on to God's promises, never wavering in their faith; and because of that, they were able to see the fruit of their faithfulness. They are all conquerors of domestic violence and are living productive lives that glorify God. Nancy and Debbie remarried and have relationships that are based on mutual love and respect for one another. Susan reconciled, after the willingness of her husband to seek help, change, and do the intensive work to heal. Now, they both have the desire for God to use their lives to help other married couples to have hope that God can transform their troubled marriages as he transformed theirs. Edith has the passion to use her life as a testimony to bring other abused Christian women to the ultimate conqueror and healer of domestic violence. It is truly amazing to witness the power of God changing lives!

NOTES

Chapter 1
1. Patricia Evans, *Verbal Abuse Survivors Speak Out: On Relationship and Recovery* (Avon: Adams Media Corporation, 1993), 44–45.
2. Cooper-White, Pamela. *Women Healing and Empowering.* (Chicago: Evangelical Lutheran Church in America, 1996), 24.

Chapter 2
1. "Violence against Women," World Health Organization Fact Sheet, http://www.who.int/mediacentre/factsheets/fs239/en/ (Accessed September 15, 2015).
2. K.J. Wilson, *When Violence Begins at Home: A Comprehensive Guide to Understanding and Ending Domestic Abuse* (Alameda: Hunter House, 1997), 8.
3. Ibid., 8–12.
4. "What Is Domestic Violence?" Maryland Network Against Domestic Violence. (Accessed August 30, 2012), http://mnadv.org/about-domestic-violence/what-is-domestic-violence/.
5. Wilson, 12.
6. M.K. Dugan and R.R. Hock, *It's My Life Now: Starting Over After an Abusive Relationship or Domestic Violence* (New York: Routledge, 2000), 10–11.
7. "Power and Control Wheel." Digital image. www.theduluthmodel.org. Used by permission.
8. Lenore E Walker, *The Battered Woman* (New York: Harper/Colophon, 1980), 56–70.
9. "What Is Domestic Violence?" http://mnadv.org/about-domestic-violence/what-is-domestic-violence/.

10. "What Is Domestic Violence?" http://mnadv.org/about-domestic-violence/what-is-domestic-violence/.
11. "What Is Domestic Violence?" http://mnadv.org/about-domestic-violence/what-is-domestic-violence/.
12. Pamela Cooper-White, *Women Healing and Empowering* (Chicago: Evangelical Lutheran Church in America, 1996), 5.
13. Ibid., 19.
14. J.C. Campbell, "Health consequences of intimate partner violence," *The Lancet*, 359 (2002), 1331–1336.
15. H. Berman, "Stories of growing up amid violence by refugee children of war and children of battered women living in Canada," *The Journal of Nursing Scholarship*, 31 (1999), 57–63.
16. S. Vitanza, L.C. Vogel and L.L Marshall, "Distress and Symptoms of Posttraumatic Stress Disorder in Abused Women," *Violence and Victims* 10, (1995).
17. Walker, 47.
18. Catherine Clark Kroeger and Nancy Nason-Clark, *No Place for Abuse. Biblical & Practical Resources to Counteract Domestic Violence* (Downers Grove, IL: InterVarsity Press, 2001), 35.
19. O.W. Barnett, "Why Battered Women Do Not Leave, Part 1: External Inhibiting Factors within Society." *Trauma, Violence, and Abuse*, 1 (2000), 343–372.
20. Cooper-White, 20.
21. Walker, 56.
22. Liz Brody, "Why Women Stay in Abusive Relationships." Glamour.com. http://www.glamour.com/sex-love-life/blogs/smitten/2011/06/why-women-stay-in-abusive-rela (Accessed September 14, 2015).
23. The National Coalition Against Domestic Violence. http://www.ncadv.org.
24. Anne Ganley and Margaret Hobart, *Social Worker's Practice Guide to Domestic Violence*. 63–65. http://nrccps.org/wp-content/uploads/WA-state-SW-DV-practice-guide-2010.pdf (Accessed September 27, 2012).

Notes

Chapter 3
1. Wilson, 181.
2. Marie M. Fortune, *Keeping the Faith: Guidance for Christian Women Facing Abuse* (San Francisco: Harper, 1995), 47.
3. Ibid., 18–20.
4. Clark Kroeger and Nancy Nason-Clark, 95.
5. Ibid., 97.
6. Ibid., 93.
7. Fortune, 38–39.
8. Clark Kroeger and Nason-Clark, 131.

Chapter 4
1. Lundy Bancroft, *Why Does He Do That? Inside the Minds of Angry and Controlling Men* (New York: Berkley Publishing Group, 2002), 21.
2. Clark Kroeger and Nancy Nason-Clark, 98.

Chapter 5
1. The National Coalition Against Domestic Violence. http://www.ncadv.org.
2. Walker, 48–50.

Chapter 6
1. Jef Gazley, "What Is Healthy Love?" Ask the Internet Therapist, http://www.asktheinternettherapist.com/articles/what-is-health love (Accessed September 14, 2015).

Chapter 7
1. Christi Ammer, *The American Heritage Dictionary of Idioms* (Boston: Houghton Mifflin, 1997).
2. M.S. Goodman and B.C. Fallon, *Pattern Changing for Abused Women: An Educational Program* (Thousand Oaks, CA: SAGE Publications, 1995), 101.
3. Ibid.,102.

4. Charles L. Whitfield, M.D., *Healing the Child Within: Discovery and Recovery for Adult Children of Dysfunctional Families* (Deerfield Beach, FL: Health Communications, 1987), 100–101.
5. Goodman and Fallon, 101–102.
6. Cooper-White, 5.
7. Goodman and Fallon, 102–103.
8. "Anger—How it Affects People," Better Health Channel, http://www.betterhealth.vic.gov.au/bhcv2/bhcarticles.nsf/pages/Anger_how_it_affects_people (Accessed September 14, 2015).
9. Clark Kroeger and Nason-Clark. 115.
10. Cooper-White, 14.
11. Ibid., 24.
12. Kendra Cherry, "Defense Mechanisms," http://psychology.about.com/od/theoriesofpersonality/ss/defensemech.htm (Accessed September 14, 2015).
13. Cooper-White, 24.
14. Ibid., 20.
15. Ibid., 24.
16. Ibid., 24.
17. Clark Kroeger and Nason-Clark, 114.
18. David Seamands and Beth Funk, *Healing for Damaged Emptions* (Colorado Springs: David C. Cook, 2001), 96.
19. Clark Kroeger and Nason-Clark, 115.
20. Ibid., 115.
21. Cooper-White, 26.
22. Clark Kroeger and Nason-Clark, 115.
23. J.W. James and R. Friedman, *The Grief Recovery Handbook: The Action Program for Moving Beyond Death, Divorce, and Other Losses including Health, Career, and Faith* (New York: HarperCollins, 2009), 3.
24. Cooper-White, 28.
25. http://www.medicinenet.com/loss_grief_and_bereavement/article.htm.
26. Whitfield, 85.
27. Ibid., 86.
28. http://www.smart-relationships.com/content/view/19/29_.

Notes

29. Cooper-White, 30.
30. Ibid., 28.
31. James and Friedman, 14–15.
32. Whitfield, 91–92.
33. Cooper-White, 29.
34. Ibid., 30-31.

Chapter 8

1. Cooper-White, 11.
2. Ibid., 11.
3. Patricia Tjaden, and Nancy Thoennes, "Extent, Nature and Consequences of Intimate Partner Violence: Findings from the National Violence Against Women Survey," National Institute of Justice and the Centers of Disease Control and Prevention (2000).
4. *Costs of Intimate Partner Violence Against Women in the United States*, Centers for Disease Control and Prevention, National Centers for Injury Prevention and Control. Atlanta, GA, 2003 http://www.cdc.gov/violenceprevention/pdf/IPVBook-a.pdf (Accessed September 14, 2015).
5. Cooper-White, 12.
6. Walker, 2.
7. N.S. Jacobson, et al. "Psychological factors in the longitudinal course of battering: when do the couples split up? when does the abuse decrease?" *Violence and Victims* 11 (1996): 371–92.
8. *Costs of Intimate Partner Violence Against Women in the United States*.
9. Ganley and Hobart, 63–65.
10. Michele Bloomquist, "Domestic Abuse: Recognizing the Potential Abuser," April 24, 2000. http://women.webmd.com/features/domestic-abuse-recognizing-potential-abuser (Accessed September 14, 2015).
11. Ibid.
12. Dugan and Hock, 218.
13. Fortune, 25.

Chapter 9

1. "US History of Marital Rape." Basic Information about Martial/Partner Rape. http://www.crisisconnectioninc.org/pdf/US_History_of_Marital_Rape.pdf (Accessed September 27, 2012).
2. "Marital/Partner Rape," WomensLaw.com http://www.womenslaw.org/laws_state_type.php?id=13226&state_code=PG#content-13230 (Accessed September 30, 2012).
3. D. Barker and Colin Padfield, *The Law Made Simple* (Bungay, Suffolk, England: The Chaucer Press, 1981).
4. "US History of Marital Rape."
5. Barker and Padfield.

RESOURCES

National Resources
The National Coalition Against Domestic Violence (www.nacadv.org)
National Domestic Violence Hotline for the United States (800) 799-7233 or TTY-800-787-3224

Helpful Books
Wilson, K.J. *When Violence Begins at Home: A Comprehensive Guide to Understanding and Ending Domestic Abuse.* Alameda, CA: Hunter House, 1997.
Bancroft, L. *Why Does He Do That? Inside the Minds of Angry and Controlling Men.* Berkley: Berkley Publishing Group, 2003.
Fortune, M.M. *Keeping the Faith: Guidance for Christian Women Facing Abuse.* San Francisco: Harper, 1995.
Miles, A. *Domestic Violence: What Every Pastor Needs to Know.* Minneapolis: Augsburg Fortress, 2000.
Dugan, M.K. & Hock, R.R. *It's My Life Now: Starting Over After an Abusive Relationship or Domestic Violence.* New York: Routledge, 2000.
Evans, P. *The Verbally Abusive Relationship: How to Recognize It and How to Respond.* Avon, MA: Adams Media Corporation, 1996.
Clark Kroeger, C., & N. Nason-Clark., *No Place for Abuse: Biblical & Practical Resources to Counteract Domestic Violence.* Downers Grove, IL: InterVarsity Press, 2001.

Videos
"Broken Vows: Religious Perspectives on Domestic Violence."
"Wings Like a Dove: Healing for the Abused Christian Woman."

CONNECT WITH THE AUTHOR:

RoseSaad.com

CPSIA information can be obtained
at www.ICGtesting.com
Printed in the USA
FFOW01n1122030616
24677FF